I0411516

Delaware Bay Shorebird-Horseshoe Crab Assessment Report and Peer Review

Prepared for the

Atlantic States Marine Fisheries Commission

by the

U.S. Fish and Wildlife Service

Shorebird Technical Committee

Peer Review Panel

June 2003

Information in the report was compiled by Brad A. Andres and available from U. S. Fish and Wildlife Service, Division of Migratory Bird Management, 4401 N. Fairfax Dr., MBSP 4107, Arlington, VA, 22203, USA or at http://migratorybirds.fws.gov/reports/reports.html

Report authors are listed in the Literature Cited. Some sections were drafted by Nellie Tsipoura (Rutgers University), Joanna Burger (Rutgers University), Gregory Breese (U. S. Fish and Wildlife Service), and Kimberly Cole (Delaware Coastal Management Programs). Shorebird Technical Committee members provided review.

Suggested citation: U.S. Fish and Wildlife Service. 2003. Delaware Bay Shorebird-Horseshoe Crab Assessment Report and Peer Review. U.S. Fish and Wildlife Service Migratory Bird Publication R9-03/02. Arlington, VA. 99 p.

TABLE OF CONTENTS

A. Conclusions, Recommendations, and Peer Review 1

   1.0. PURPOSE AND APPROACH 1

   2.0. LONG-DISTANCE MIGRATION IN SHOREBIRDS 1

   3.0. CONCLUSIONS..2
      3.1. Shorebird Use of Delaware Bay 2
      3.2. Shorebird Population Trends 2
      3.3. Shorebird Population Threats 3
      3.4. Shorebird Use of Horseshoe Crab Eggs...4
      3.5. Availability of Horseshoe Crab Eggs 4
      3.6. Shorebird Weight Gain in Delaware Bay 5
      3.7. Shorebird Survival 6

   4.0. RECOMMENDATIONS..7
      4.1. Direct Management..8
          4.1.1. Horseshoe crab egg abundance..8
          4.1.2. Seasonal beach closures..8
          4.1.3. Habitat protection and enhancement......................................8
      4.3. Needed Analyses..10
          4.2.1. Horseshoe crab egg abundance..9
          4.2.2. Shorebird breeding-ground conditions 9
          4.2.3. Shorebird diet and energetics..9
      4.3. Improved Monitoring and Research 10
          4.3.1. Bay-wide horseshoe crab egg abundance 10
          4.3.2. Shorebird population surveys 10
          4.3.2. Individually-marked shorebirds..10
          4.3.4. Measurements of weight gain...10
          4.3.5. Southern stop over quality 10

   5.0. SHOREBIRD TECHNICAL COMMITTEE MEMBERSHIP 11

   6.0. PEER REVIEW PANEL PARTICIPANTS 11

B. Shorebird-Horseshoe Crab Assessment 12

1.0. INTRODUCTION 12
      1.1. Shorebird Technical Committee 12
      1.2. Horseshoe Crabs, Shorebirds, and Delaware Bay 12

1.3. Economic Value of Crabs and Shorebirds...13
1.4. Evaluation Approach 13

2.0. DELAWARE BAY SHOREBIRDS...14
2.1. Species Considered 14
2.2. Conservation Status and Protection 14
2.3. Vulnerability of Long-distance Migrant Shorebirds and the Red Knot Focus15
2.4. Red Knot Distribution..15
2.5. Red Knot Annual Cycle 15
2.6. Distribution and Migration Routes of Other Species...16
    2.6.1. Ruddy turnstone 16
    2.6.2. Sanderling 17
    2.6.3. Semipalmated sandpiper 17
    2.6.4. Dunlin 17
    2.6.5. Short-billed dowitcher 17
    2.6.6. Long-billed dowitcher...18
    2.6.7. Least sandpiper 18

3.0. ABUNDANCE AND DISTRIBUTION OF HORSESHOE CRABS 18

4.0. POTENTIAL THREATS TO SHOREBIRDS 20
4.1. Heavy Metal Concentrations in Shorebirds and Horseshoe Crabs 20
4.2. Organic Compound Concentrations in Shorebirds and Horseshoe Crabs 21
4.3. Disease in Shorebirds...22
4.4. Shoreline Changes in Delaware Bay..23
4.5. Sea Level Rise from Global Climate Change 23
4.6. Arctic Breeding Ground Conditions 23
4.7. South American Wintering Ground Conditions 25
4.8. Human Disturbance to Shorebirds...25
4.9. Effect of Disturbance on Survival of Semipalmated Sandpipers...............26
4.10. Horseshoe Crab Bait Landings 27
4.11. Changes in Horseshoe Crab Populations 27

5.0. ESTIMATES OF SHOREBIRD POPULATION SIZES AND TRENDS.............29
5.1. Shorebird Population Sizes 29
    5.1.1. Coarse continental estimates...29
    5.1.2. Re-sighting banded red knots in the 1980s.................................29
    5.1.3. Red knot band re-sighting in South America...............................30
5.2. Shorebird Population Trends 30
    5.2.1. Aerial surveys of red knots in South America...............................30
    5.2.2. Spring aerial surveys in Delaware Bay 31
    5.2.3. International and Maritime Shorebird Surveys..............................32
    5.2.4. Quebec migration checklists...32

6.0. IMPORTANCE OF DELAWARE BAY TO SHOREBIRD POPULATIONS 33

7.0. HABITAT USE BY SHOREBIRDS AND HORSESHOE CRABS.........................34
    7.1. Shorebird Use of Marine and Non-marine Habitats 34
    7.2. Red Knot Habitat Use and Movements in Delaware Bay.............................34
    7.3. Shorebird Habitat Use on Cape May Peninsula, New Jersey 34
    7.4. Shorebird Beach Use in Delaware 35
    7.5. Influence of Beach Characteristics on Horseshoe Crab Reproductive Activity35
    7.6. Beach Nourishment and Habitat Restoration for Crabs and Shorebirds 36
    7.7. Shorebird Habitat Use in Relation to Beach Characteristics and Abundance
        of Horseshoe Crabs and Their Eggs...37

8.0. ABUNDANCE AND TRENDS OF HORSESHOE CRAB EGGS 38
    8.1. Bay-wide Egg Density in 1999...38
    8.2. Egg Density on Delaware Beaches 38
    8.3. Changes in Egg Density on New Jersey Beaches 38
    8.4. Egg Abundance Sampling Design Considerations 39

9.0. SHOREBIRD DIET AND USE OF HORSESHOE CRAB EGGS.........................39
    9.1. Shorebird Diet in Delaware Bay...39
    9.2. Stable Isotope Analysis Confirms Shorebird Dependance on Horseshoe Crab
        Eggs in Delaware Bay...40
    9.3. Functional Responses of Shorebirds Feeding on Horseshoe Crab Eggs 40
    9.4. Competition Between Shorebirds and Gulls for Horseshoe Crab Eggs 41
    9.5. Red Knots Use of Food Other than Horseshoe Crab Eggs 42

10.0 ENERGETIC REQUIREMENTS OF MIGRANT SHOREBIRDS.......................43
    10.1. An Energetics Framework for Migrant Shorebirds 43
    10.2. Energetics of Sanderlings Migrating to Four Latitudes............................44
    10.3. Predicting Flight Ranges...44
    10.4. Fat-loading in *islandica* Red Knots 45
    10.5. Effects of Weight on Metabolic Power Needed for Flight 45
    10.6. Flight Energy Needs of *rufa* Red Knots Staging in Delaware Bay 46
    10.7. Assimilation Efficiency of Sanderlings Consuming Horseshoe Crab Eggs 46
    10.8. Energy budget of Delaware Bay Shorebirds..47
    10.9. Horseshoe Crab Egg Requirement of Delaware Bay Shorebirds 47

11.0. SHOREBIRD WEIGHTS AND WEIGHT GAIN 48
    11.1. General Capture Methods 48
    11.2. Organ Atrophy and Weight Change during Migration..............................49
    11.3. Red Knot Weights through the Annual Cycle 50
    11.4. Red Knot Weight Gains in Delaware Bay 51
        11.4.1. Analytical approaches...51
        11.4.2. Red knot arrival weights and weight gains 51

11.4.3. Red knot departure weights in Delaware Bay...............................53
11.5. Weights and Weight Gain in Ruddy Turnstones and Sanderlings...............53
11.6. Weights and Weight Gain in Semipalmated and Least Sandpipers............54

12.0. RED KNOT SURVIVAL AND PRODUCTIVITY 55
12.1. Re-sighting Rates of Knots Banded in Florida and Argentina 55
12.2. Survival Rate..55
12.3. Population Projections 56
12.4. Juvenile Age Ratios 56

13.0. LITERATURE CITED 57

14.0. TABLES 72

15.0. FIGURES...91

C. Shorebird Technical Committee Terms of Reference – 2002 94

A. Conclusions, Recommendations, and Peer Review

1.0. PURPOSE AND APPROACH

The Atlantic States Marine Fisheries Commission asked the U. S. Fish and Wildlife Service to form a Shorebird Technical Committee that would provide technical guidance, regarding effects that horseshoe crab management actions could have on shorebird populations, to the Horseshoe Crab Management Board. One of the immediate tasks of the Shorebird Technical Committee was to produce a peer-reviewed report that synthesized unpublished and published information on shorebird population trends, threats to shorebird populations, shorebird habitat use, shorebird energetic requirements, and horseshoe crab egg abundance. Although several shorebird species were considered in the report, attention primarily focused on the red knot (*Calidris canutus rufa*). Available information was greatest for the red knot and was less extensive for the ruddy turnstone (*Arenaria interpres morinella*), sanderling (*Calidris alba*), semipalmated sandpiper (*Calidris pusilla*), and least sandpiper (*Calidris minutilla*). Relatively little information existed on the dunlin (*Calidris alpina hudsonia*) and short-billed dowitcher (*Limnodromus griseus griseus*). Aside from the least sandpiper, which was chosen because of its contrasting use of marsh habitats, all other species were selected because of their reliance on beach habitats and their frequency of occurrence on Delaware Bay aerial surveys (1986–2002). After reviewing the report, the Committee has generated this set of conclusions, management recommendations, and information needs. The Committee used a concordance, or preponderance, of evidence approach to evaluate the report's contents. The report, conclusions, and recommendations were evaluated by an independent Peer Review Panel, and their comments are included here as bolded text.

2.0. LONG-DISTANCE MIGRATION IN SHOREBIRDS

Many populations of shorebirds undertake a series of long-distance, non-stop flights to travel between their wintering and breeding grounds. Because a shorebird often crosses vast stretches of open water during migration, physiological and environmental conditions on departure can directly, and immediately, affect its survival. The red knot is an extreme example of the long-hop migration system and has one of the longest migrations of any bird. Besides adding 50% of their body weight in fat reserves, red knots at Delaware Bay, and elsewhere, exhibit major internal organ changes in response to the need to first accumulate fat and later to reduce flight mass. The long-hop migration system of red knots, and other shorebird species, is highly dependent on food availability at a limited number of stopover sites. Failure to gain sufficient body mass at stopover sites, often during a short time span, can impair the health, productivity, and survival of migrant shorebirds. Because arctic breeding grounds are generally food limited in early summer when shorebirds first arrive, food-rich stopovers in the north-temperate region are particularly important. At these sites, shorebirds are often under relatively strict time constraints to add needed fat reserves.

3.0. CONCLUSIONS

3.1. Shorebird Use of Delaware Bay

Delaware Bay has been recognized by many scientists and organizations as one of the most important and critical shorebird stopovers in the Western Hemisphere and, indeed, in the world. Depending on the species, between 12 and 80% of the Atlantic flyway population of the six beach-inhabiting shorebirds mentioned above (excluding least sandpiper) can be observed on Delaware Bay's beaches during northward migration. Far fewer numbers of shorebirds pass through Delaware Bay during southward migration. For a given species, the proportion of the population that uses Delaware Bay each spring may vary substantially among years. Compared to 1986–1996, average shorebird use of Delaware Bay beaches, as measured by seasonal maxima of aerial survey counts, has increased or remained stable during 1997–2002 for all six beach-inhabiting species. During their northward migration in the Delaware Bay region, most shorebird species use marine-influenced habitats — either salt marshes, tidal flats, or sand beaches.

The Peer Review Panel generally agrees with these conclusions, except that a more sophisticated analysis of the Delaware Bay shorebird use time-series data could have been conducted. Data on shorebird-use days could be useful in constructing a total energy budget for all northward-migrating shorebirds. The importance of accessible roosting sites to migrant shorebirds is not mentioned.

3.2. Shorebird Population Trends

Based on a variety of sources, all available data indicate that the *rufa* red knot population has decreased since the 1980s, but the magnitude of the decline is not precisely known. Besides the red knot, the semipalmated sandpiper is the only other Delaware Bay shorebird species that has relatively consistent patterns of population decreases among trend datasets. Because of unknown turnover and detection rates, aerial survey data from Delaware Bay are not useful for estimating population sizes of shorebirds in Delaware Bay.

The Peer Review Panel agrees that, although imperfect, patterns in the trend analyses reasonably indicate a decrease, of some magnitude, in populations of *rufa* red knots and semipalmated sandpipers. Most surveys of wintering and migrating red knots do not cover the needed range of the population and complicate interpretation of changes in populations at specific sites. Analytical methods used to summarize ISS data also lack rigor and may only reveal general patterns of population change. Current and future surveys of shorebird populations should undergo rigorous statistical review.

3.3. Shorebird Population Threats

The Shorebird Technical Committee evaluated information on the potential threats to shorebird populations across their annual cycle. Testing for contaminants in shorebirds and crabs indicates that metals and pesticides are not likely causing population reductions in shorebirds. Little information exists on disease and parasite occurrence in red knots, particularly in Delaware Bay, but there is no current evidence to suggest that these are major, potential problems. Although environmental conditions vary considerably from year to year, arctic breeding habitats do not appear to have changed in ways that would likely contribute to the observed reductions in red knot survival and productivity. More information is needed to assess the effects that weather and predation in the arctic have on *rufa* red knot population dynamics. Arctic environmental conditions should also be evaluated for semipalmated sandpipers. Habitat conditions in wintering areas have numerous potential threats, but these are not believed to have currently affected key wintering sites. Food availability, however, has only been measured at a few South American wintering or stopover sites. Beach nourishment is not having a negative effect on shorebird use on Delaware beaches and is likely improving habitat quality; beach nourishment is not widely practiced in New Jersey. Although no Bay-specific studies have been conducted, repeated human disturbance likely reduces shorebird feeding efficiency in Delaware Bay. Elsewhere, migrant shorebirds have been disturbed by dogs, self-propelled human recreation, and vehicles. Human disturbance to semipalmated sandpipers feeding along the coast of Massachusetts as they prepared for a long over-water flight, reduced their subsequent survival. Gulls can potentially reduce food availability to shorebirds through direct and indirect competition for crab eggs. Shorebirds, however, most often forage with other shorebirds, and preliminary data and field observations suggest that the number of gulls using Delaware Bay beaches has not substantially increased in recent years. Lastly, reduced numbers of horseshoe crab eggs available for shorebird consumption, relative to the early 1990s, could reduce survival and reproductive success in the six shorebird species that use Delaware Bay as the last stopover prior to departing for their breeding grounds (see following sections).

The Peer Review Panel agrees that contaminants and parasites do not currently appear to provide a major threat to shorebirds stopping at Delaware Bay. Further information is needed to thoroughly evaluate whether or not changes in habitat quality on the breeding and wintering grounds are contributing to declines in shorebird populations. However, changes in breeding or wintering area conditions do not minimize the importance of maintaining high quality north-temperate stopovers. Information presented in the report is insufficient to determine if beach nourishment generally improves habitat quality for spawning horseshoe crabs and foraging shorebirds. Although numerous studies have demonstrated the immediate, disruptive effects of human disturbance to migrant shorebirds, ultimate effects of disturbance on survival of shorebirds are not well-documented and are usually inferred (including the Massachusetts semipalmated sandpiper study referenced above). Increases in gull numbers do not superficially appear to have direct or indirect influences on shorebird population changes, but more quantitative information on effects of interference and exploitative competition between

gulls and shorebirds is needed. The life history of long-distance, long-hop shorebird migrants indicates that the availability of abundant food resources at north-temperate stopovers is critical for completing their annual cycle.

3.4. Shorebird Use of Horseshoe Crab Eggs

The importance of Delaware Bay as a spring shorebird stopover is likely due to the unique and important food resource — horseshoe crab eggs. A variety of methods (stomach analyses, captive feeding studies, and field observations) indicate that horseshoe crab eggs are a variable component in the diet of numerous invertebrates and vertebrates (shorebirds, other birds, fish, and turtles). Birds, and particularly shorebirds, are important predators of crab eggs. Stable isotope analysis indicates that red knots are highly dependent on horseshoe crab eggs. Isotope analysis of other shorebird species is currently underway. Red knots feed by pecking at surface eggs and making shallow probes into beach sediments. Captive knots fed exclusively eggs gained weight at rates that were similar to those observed in wild birds. Egg consumption was estimated at 18,000 eggs per day and rates of knot weight gain ranged from 2.6 to 8.0 grams per day while they were in Delaware Bay. Daily weight gains of *rufa* red knots in Delaware Bay are the highest reported for any stopover site or knot population. At other stopovers throughout the world, knots generally feed on molluscs or bivalves. Although Bay beaches were reported to have low invertebrate prey densities, detailed evidence does not exist to thoroughly evaluate whether or not alternative shorebird foods exist in high enough abundances to meet the energetic needs of red knots and other migrant shorebirds while in the Delaware Bay region.

The Peer Review Panel believes that the importance of Delaware Bay to shorebirds is due to a number of factors such as an abundant primary food resource (crab eggs), the availability of secondary food resources, and availability of safe roost sites. Stable isotope analysis indicates that red knots feed almost exclusively on horseshoe crabs while at Delaware Bay. Although this result does not necessarily indicate a "dependency" on this food, crabs should be assumed to be critically important unless a viable alternative prey base is shown to exist. A comprehensive review of migrant shorebird foraging behavior and diet is needed to thoroughly evaluate the importance of Delaware Bay, and its food resources, to shorebirds; caloric value of alternative foods should be determined. No information was presented on the specific egg or larval life stage was being consumed by shorebirds. Foraging behavior of knots, in particular, at sites other than Delaware Bay could provide insights into the importance of the Bay's horseshoe crabs to shorebirds. The habitat section of the report should have included more information, if available, on the correlation between beach use by shorebirds and the distribution of horseshoe crab spawning females and eggs.

3.5. Availability of Horseshoe Crab Eggs

Although a sampling plan has been devised, no Bay-wide, systematic survey of egg availability has yet been conducted. Geographically limited surveys conducted in May, variably over the last four years, do not provide conclusive evidence of a trend in the abundance of surface eggs available to shorebirds. Likewise, there are not ample data to assess whether or not surface horseshoe crab eggs occur in abundances that will support Delaware Bay populations of migrant shorebirds. Although counts of spawning crabs have not changed between 1999 and 2002, trawl survey indices of all age-classes of crabs are now lower than they were in the early 1990s. Further analysis of egg data collected on New Jersey beaches and additional information on the temporal and spatial distribution of surface and sub-surface eggs is needed to thoroughly evaluate if there has been a significant trend in horseshoe crab egg abundance. Further refinement of the total shorebird energy budget is needed to determine how many eggs are required across the entire spring season.

The Peer Review Panel believes that knowledge about the spatial and temporal patterns of horseshoe crab egg densities is critical to understanding how crab management affects migrant shorebird populations. Specifically, a clearer understanding of how eggs become available to shorebirds is needed. Energetic considerations indicate that horseshoe crab eggs are only profitable to shorebirds if they occur in high surface densities. The excavation and transport of eggs to the beach surface might only occur when spawning females occur in very high densities, and there may be a threshold female crab density at which sufficient numbers of eggs become available on the surface. Little appears to be known about the depletion of surface eggs attributable to shorebird, and other bird, predation. Depletion of surface eggs would be consistent with the hypothesis that crab eggs are a limiting resource for shorebirds. The Panel agrees that information from trawl surveys, given gear limitations for adequately sampling large numbers of crabs, indicates that horseshoe crabs in Delaware Bay are currently at lower levels than they were in the early 1990s. Uncertainty in recent estimates of sizes of horseshoe crab age classes precludes reasonable comparison of recruitment rates and harvest levels. The report would have benefitted from thorough analyses of datasets already collected on changes in egg densities on New Jersey beaches. An unified bioenergetics model for Delaware Bay shorebirds will be needed to integrate the information about available food with the requirements of shorebirds.

3.6. Shorebird Weight Gain in Delaware Bay

There is agreement that a smaller percentage of *rufa* red knots are making threshold departure weights by the end of May in recent years. These results are not dependent on inclusion of 1997, a year when shorebird-banding did not begin until 22 May. The different analytical approaches used to determine weight gains of Delaware Bay red knots (average weights of time-dependent catches, cohort analysis, and individual recaptures) have generated two hypotheses regarding decreases in rates of weight gain between 1997 and 2002 — either a greater proportion of red knots are arriving later in Delaware Bay in recent years, or red knots are increasingly unable to find sufficient food. In the first analytical approach, rates of weight gain in knots decreased through time, but in the latter two approaches they did not. Evidence suggests that rates of weight gain by semipalmated sandpipers have decreased in recent years, while rates of weight gain in least sandpipers, a more marsh-foraging species, remained stable. Patterns of decreasing (average) rates of weight gain were less consistent for ruddy turnstones and were not apparent in sanderlings. Ruddy turnstones can excavate eggs to feed on, and sanderlings are thought to commute regularly between Atlantic Ocean and Delaware Bay feeding sites. No hypotheses, as an alternative to decreased horseshoe crab egg availability, have been formulated to explain changes found in weight gains of semipalmated sandpipers. Semipalmated sandpipers do not winter in the same regions of South America as red knots. More information on the condition of South American stopovers and observations of individually marked birds are needed to fully discriminate between these two alternatives. Late arrival of knots could be caused by changes in spring weather patterns or by their inability to build fat stores at South American stopovers. Red knots can physiologically compensate for late arrival by increasing their rates of fat deposition while in Delaware Bay.

The Peer Review Panel believes that the two hypotheses forwarded to explain changes in weight gain in Delaware Bay red knots are not mutually exclusive, but instead represent two factors which operate in tandem to affect departure weights from Delaware Bay. Both factors operate within the same year, although their relative importance may vary among years. The existing data, however, are not adequate to evaluate their relative importance for any year of record. But in any case, Delaware Bay must provide the food resources shorebirds need to adequately gain fat mass to make the flight to the arctic. That a lesser proportion of red knots are making minimal departure weights suggests that food resources in Delaware Bay may not be adequate. Similar feeding rates observed among species of different size supports the finding that the larger red knots should be most sensitive to decreases in food availability. The shorebird banding program in Delaware Bay would greatly benefit by a more cooperative approach to design and analysis. Procedures used in both analyses of weight gain were not documented adequately enough in supporting reports to allow independent evaluation. Patterns of weight gain were more clearly presented for semipalmated and least sandpipers. Unfortunately, attempts to estimate growth rate based on independent samples of body mass are inherently flawed, as assumptions must be made to accommodate the uncertainty in arrival times of birds. These assumptions lead to the possibility of conflicting results and additional controversy. Adjusting field methods to emphasize the collection of multiple measurements on individual birds would increase the sample of individually-marked birds and would ultimately strengthen conclusions about annual changes in rates of weight gain.

3.7. Shorebird Survival

Shorebird return rates (on southward migration) relative to stopover departure weights indicate that the inability to gain sufficient weight at stopover sites can reduce survivorship for red knots (*Calidris canutus*) and semipalmated sandpipers (*Calidris pusilla*), which supports the link between stopover conditions and population trends. Recent estimates of adult survival and productivity of *rufa* red knots are substantially lower than estimates for knot populations wintering in Europe and Australia; these knot populations also breed in arctic regions and undertake long-distance, long-hop migrations. Sustained low levels of vital rates could cause a drastic decline in the knot population. Evidence generated through population modeling, however, was insufficient to evaluate the probabilities of extinction under the current range of demographic values.

The Peer Review Panel supports the conclusion that low-weight red knots had a lower return rate, but found the estimates of adult survival to be highly variable among periods. Further details of the analytical procedures used for estimating survival rates are needed to thoroughly evaluate these results for application to management decisions. To fully evaluate the biological significance of survival rates and juvenile ratios, better information on non-breeding distribution and movements of juveniles is needed. Because estimates among years were from different sites, the variability of these estimates among sites should be evaluated. Overall, the Panel believes that design and analysis of future mark-resight/ recapture studies could be improved to remove ambiguities in interpretation of results and to take better
advantage of the large number of banded birds. Use of field-readable, individually-numbered color flags should be thoroughly evaluated.

4.0. RECOMMENDATIONS

Horseshoe crab management actions already taken (for example, bait bags, harvest reductions, alternative bait development, designation of the Carl N. Shuster, Jr. Horseshoe Crab Reserve) have likely improved conservation of crabs and shorebirds. Despite these actions, and the stability of spawning horseshoe crab numbers over the last four years, the population of red knots, and perhaps other species, has declined. As a general management action, the U. S. Shorebird Conservation Plan suggests that any declining shorebird population should be stabilized and then restored to population levels of the late 1970s and early 1980s. Accordingly, shorebirds in Delaware Bay should be managed to maintain current population sizes, and decreasing populations should be stabilized and then increased.

Based on the shorebird and crab information currently available, the Shorebird Technical Committee therefore recommends that the Horseshoe Crab Management Board pursue a management strategy that is more risk-averse to shorebirds. Using an adaptive approach, continued or improved monitoring programs for shorebirds, horseshoe crabs, and horseshoe crab eggs are needed to evaluate results of management actions and to provide guidance for future selection of management alternatives. The Shorebird Technical Committee supports the cooperative effort of the Horseshoe Crab Technical Committee and the Horseshoe Crab Stock Assessment Committee to develop and implement various crab surveys. Specific recommendations of the Shorebird Technical Committee follow, which were generally supported by all Committee members. Peer Review Panel comments are also included, as bolded text, below.

4.1. Direct Management

4.1.1. Horseshoe crab egg abundance

Until further information is available on whether or not current egg abundances are sufficient for shorebirds to reach threshold departure weights, the Committee recommends further reductions in bait landings for New Jersey, Delaware, and Maryland. Although the Committee realizes there currently are no biological reference points on which to base reduction amounts, total reductions in the range of 50 to 75% below the Reference Period Landings might be considered. Committee members could not reach consensus on the amount of reduction, if any, that would be considered risk-averse. Because crabs caught in Federal waters from New York and to Virginia ca be landed in any of the mid-Atlantic states, in New York and Virginia might also be considered. Mandatory use of bait bags and development of alternative baits could contribute to reduced bait use of horseshoe crabs.

The Peer Review Panel supports a reduction in harvest but suggests that this action be viewed as an interim solution until integrated and comprehensive models are constructed to set reasonable biological objectives for shorebirds. Although the Panel is unsure about the amount of the reduction that is immediately needed, the numerous indications of shorebird population declines suggests that harvest rates should be at or below the current levels. Based on very limited data, a 75% reduction would ensure recruitment of female crabs into the breeding population at the low bound of the population estimate of primiparus female crab; a 66% reduction would allow no population growth at this level. Development of conservation methods to use bait crabs most efficiently is worthwhile. Landings in states other than New Jersey, Delaware, and Maryland should be carefully tracked.

4.1.2. Seasonal beach closures

To increase abundance and availability of horseshoe crab eggs for feeding shorebirds, restrict hand harvest of horseshoe crabs, vehicles, humans, and dogs on State- and Federally-owned beaches important to shorebirds from 1 May to 7 June, the period of highest shorebird use, along the Delaware Bay shoreline of Delaware and New Jersey. Evaluate the effectiveness of restrictions.

The Peer Review Panel believes that this is a reasonable short-term action to increase the number of horseshoe crab eggs available to migrant shorebirds. Evaluation of these restrictive measures should be undertaken.

4.1.3. Habitat protection and enhancement

Encourage Delaware and New Jersey to continue environmentally responsible beach nourishment and other enhancement projects that increase high quality habitat for spawning crabs and feeding shorebirds. Consider long-term protection measures, including easements and acquisition, for beaches that are important for crab spawning and shorebird foraging. Evaluate the effectiveness of beach enhancement activities.

The Peer Review Panel believes further evaluation of the effects of beach nourishment on horseshoe crab spawning and invertebrate infauna are warranted before broad-scale activities are undertaken. If results of these evaluations, preferably using a before-and-after experimental design, are favorable, specific prescriptions of "environmentally responsible" practices should be developed. Evaluations and prescriptions should be sensitive to the geographic scale of application. Long-term protection of beaches would likely be a beneficial conservation measure.

4.2. Needed Analyses

4.2.1. Horseshoe crab egg abundance

Complete analyses of horseshoe crab egg abundance data that have already been collected on New Jersey beaches to further evaluate evidence of a change in egg abundance.

4.2.2. Shorebird breeding-ground conditions

Compile information on annual weather conditions and predation pressure on breeding grounds to assess short- and long-term effects on red knot survival and reproduction and on semipalmated sandpiper population change. Report information on density, hatching success, and habitat use on breeding grounds.

4.2.3. Shorebird diet and energetics

Complete stable isotope analysis for remaining Delaware Bay shorebird species to quantify their dependence on horseshoe crab eggs. Develop the best possible estimate of the total energy needed and horseshoe crab eggs required by all migrant Delaware Bay shorebirds. Complete analysis of information on alternative foods available to Delaware Bay shorebirds to determine if other energy sources exist that could supplement horseshoe crab eggs. Report on role of nocturnal foraging.

The Peer Review Panel encourages efforts to expedite the reporting and analysis of all previously-collected data pertinent to topics addressed in the report. The Panel also encourages the involvement of biometricians in these analyses.

4.3. Improved Monitoring and Research

4.3.1. Bay-wide horseshoe crab egg abundance

Support implementation of the Bay-wide egg survey to determine abundance of, and ultimately trend in, horseshoe crab eggs on Delaware Bay beaches. Information is needed on egg deposition and movements to understand what makes eggs available to shorebirds on Delaware Bay beaches.

4.3.2. Shorebird population surveys

Continue, and expand, the aerial survey of South American wintering grounds of red knots to identify additional concentration areas and track population changes. Include areas with winter aggregations of semipalmated sandpipers. Develop and evaluate other counting and demographic methods to track populations of shorebirds.

4.3.3. Individually-marked shorebirds

Increase marking and scan-sampling of red knots on wintering grounds and in Delaware Bay to track changes in population size, annual survival, and reproductive success. Expand efforts to include semipalmated sandpipers. Use individually color-flagged and radio-tagged shorebirds to determine movements into and within Delaware Bay to evaluate the late-arrival hypothesis.

4.3.4. Measurements of weight gain

Continue to monitor shorebird weights in Delaware Bay, while minimizing disturbance to foraging shorebirds. Agree on standard data collection techniques, for both sides of Delaware Bay, and record wing length and time after capture that weighing takes place. Develop a common, Bay-wide database and agree on analytical approaches.

4.3.5. Southern stop over quality

Assess habitat quality of stopovers south of Delaware Bay to determine if South American sites are providing enough food resources for migrant red knots and other shorebird species to gain the weight needed to undertake trans-ocean flights.

The Peer Review Panel believes that virtually all management, research, and monitoring programs would benefit from being placed within a more holistic and comprehensive framework in which models are used to provide coherent structure for both combining existing information and predicting consequences of management activities. Currently, many of the research and monitoring efforts are fragmented and isolated, and it is unclear whether appropriate information is presently collected to best aid management decisions. The Panel encourages the Shorebird Technical Committee to work with all partners and

stakeholders to develop a more comprehensive and integrated research and monitoring program. Theoretical models should be developed for core components of this program that would include: 1) integrated shorebird energetics and horseshoe crab egg availability, 2) shorebird demographics, and 3) monitoring design and analysis. Even in the absence of detailed quantitative information, explicit, well-developed models can illustrate the most likely explanatory hypotheses, identify speculative and real data linkages, highlight key gaps in current knowledge, and clarify specific goals and objectives. For many of the research and monitoring components, more emphasis should be placed on the use of information collected on individually-marked shorebirds, including radio-tagged birds. A premium should be placed on the development of robust survey and experimental designs.

5.0. SHOREBIRD TECHNICAL COMMITTEE MEMBERSHIP

Karen Bennett   Shorebird biologist, Delaware Division of Fish and Wildlife
Gregory Breese   Shorebird biologist, U. S. Fish and Wildlife Service
Joanna Burger   Shorebird biologist, Rutgers University
David Carter   Coastal zone manager, Delaware Coastal Management Program
Robert Gorrell   Fisheries biologist, National Marine Fisheries Service
Brian Harrington   Shorebird biologist, Manomet Center for Conservation Sciences
Marshall Howe   Shorebird biologist, U. S. Geological Survey
Stewart Michels   Fisheries biologist, Horseshoe Crab Technical Committee
Mike Millard   Fisheries biologist, U. S. Fish and Wildlife Service
David Mizrahi   Shorebird biologist, New Jersey Audubon Society
Lawrence Niles   Shorebird biologist, New Jersey Division of Fish and Wildlife
Nellie Tsipoura   Shorebird biologist, National Resource Defense Council (formerly)
Brad Andres   Coordinator, Shorebird biologist, U. S. Fish and Wildlife Service

6.0. PEER REVIEW PANEL PARTICIPANTS

Dr. H. Jane Brockmann   University of Florida, Department of Zoology
Dr. Chris S. Elphick   University of Connecticut, Department of Ecology and Evolutionary Biology
Dr. James D. Fraser   Virginia Polytechnic Institute & State University, Department of Fisheries and Wildlife Sciences
Dr. Patrick G. R. Jodice   South Carolina Cooperative Fish and Wildlife Research Unit, Clemson University
Dr. Erica Nol   Trent University, Biology Department
Dr. Adrian H. Farmer   U. S. Geological Survey, Fort Collins Science Center
Dr. James D. Nichols   U. S. Geological Survey, Patuxent Wildlife Research Center
Dr. John R. Sauer   U. S. Geological Survey, Patuxent Wildlife Research Center

B. Shorebird-Horseshoe Crab Assessment

1.0. INTRODUCTION

1.1. Shorebird Technical Committee

The Atlantic States Marine Fisheries Commission asked the U. S. Fish and Wildlife Service to form a Shorebird Technical Committee that would provide technical guidance, regarding effects that horseshoe crab management actions could have on shorebird populations, to the Horseshoe Crab Management Board. Members and Terms of Reference of this committee are provided along with this report. The immediate task of the committee is to produce a peer-reviewed report that reviews and synthesizes unpublished and published information on shorebird populations, shorebird habitat use, shorebird energetic requirements, threats to shorebird populations, and horseshoe crab egg abundance. From this report, the committee will generate a set of conclusions, management recommendations, and research needs. The report and recommendations will also undergo an independent peer review.

1.2. Horseshoe Crabs, Shorebirds, and Delaware Bay

Reported commercial landings of horseshoe crabs (*Limulus polyphemus*) on the Atlantic coast of the U. S. increased dramatically, relative to the previous 4 decades, in the mid 1990s (Figure 4 *in* Walls et al. 2002). Horseshoe crabs are most abundant between Virginia and New Jersey (Shuster 1982), and Delaware Bay supports the largest concentration of spawning individuals (Shuster and Botton 1985, Botton and Ropes 1987). Delaware Bay also supports large aggregations of shorebirds (>500,000 individuals) during spring migration and is one of the most numerically important spring stopover sites in North America (Clark et al. 1993). Timing of shorebird arrival coincides with the availability of an abundant food source — the eggs released by spawning horseshoe crabs — that is used to build fat reserves for non-stop flights to breeding grounds in the Canadian arctic (Myers 1986). Hence, concern has been raised about the negative effect that crab harvest might have on shorebirds during spring migration (see Berkson and Shuster 1999). Although several actions have recently been taken to conserve horseshoe crab populations (restrictions on harvest, delineation of a no-fishing reserve, use of bait bags, and development of alternative baits), the current status of horseshoe crabs, shorebirds, and their relationship remains unclear (see Walls et al. 2002).

1.3. Economic Value of Crabs and Shorebirds

Horseshoe crabs are commercially harvested for use in the biomedical industry (where crabs are bled and usually returned to the ocean) and as bait in the American eel (*Anguilla rostrada*) and "conch" (really a whelk, *Busycon* spp.) pot fisheries (Atlantic States Marine Fisheries Commission 1998a*). Eels are then used for either finfish bait or human consumption. An economic analysis indicates that the annual social welfare benefit (the benefit to consumers because they are able to purchase goods and services below their willingness to pay) of the fishery along the entire Atlantic coast is about $150 million for the biomedical industry and $21 million for the commercial eel and whelk fisheries (Manion et al. 2000*; 1999 dollars). Regional economic outputs (New Jersey, Delaware, Maryland) are valued (1999 dollars) at $2.2 – 2.8 million for the eel/whelk fisheries, $26.7 – 34.9 million biomedical industry, and $6.8 – $10.3 million for recreational birding (Manion et al. 2000*). Another study estimated that 6,000 – 10,000 recreational birders visited New Jersey's Delaware Bay beaches in the spring and contributed a gross economic value (total gross output + consumers' surplus) of 11.8 – 15.9 million to local communities (Eubanks et al. 2000*). Overall, the biomedical use of horseshoe crabs is the most economically valuable across the entire Atlantic coast, and the regional value of crabs to recreational birding is at least, if not greater, than the commercial value.

1.4. Evaluation Approach

Under the precautionary principle (Buhl-Mortensen and Welin 1998), Smith et al. (2002c) suggest that it would be risk prone to assume species' risk is low unless a statistical power analysis had shown that a study design was powerful enough to detect biologically meaningful change. Peterman and M'Gonigle (1992) outline 3 outcomes when statistical power is incorporated into decision-making: 1) a biologically meaningful and statistically significant decline results in harvest restrictions, 2) no evident decline and high power results in no harvest restrictions, and 3) a biologically meaningful, statistically non-significant decline and low power increases species' risk. In the latter case, high uncertainty should trigger harvest restrictions as a risk-averse strategy. Power analyses generally address singular datasets. To judge an overall effect when multiple studies or datasets test a singular null hypothesis, a concordance of evidence approach is a reasonable way to evaluate overall effects (Andres 1999). Thus, a preponderance of evidence in one direction or the other should result in clear management action (including no action). Therefore, the committee will use the concordance, or preponderance, of evidence approach described above to evaluate the report's contents. Because many regression analyses are sensitive to the time period selected, and results varied widely depending on starting year, analyses of some population data were compared among 2 groups — before 1997 and after, and including, 1997. More intensive shorebird and horseshoe crab studies were generally initiated during, or after, 1997. An "*" after the year of a citation indicates that the material is an unpublished report, a submitted manuscript, or an abstract.

2.0. DELAWARE BAY SHOREBIRDS

2.1. Species Considered

Although several shorebird species will be considered in this report, attention will primarily focus on the red knot (*Calidris canutus*). Available information is greatest for the red knot and is less extensive for the ruddy turnstone (*Arenaria interpres*), sanderling (*Calidris alba*), semipalmated sandpiper (*Calidris pusilla*), and least sandpiper (*Calidris minutilla*). Relatively little specific information exists on the dunlin (*Calidris alpina*), short-billed dowitcher (*Limnodromus griseus*), or long-billed dowitcher (*Limnodromus scolopaceus*). Information presented is specific to taxa that use Delaware Bay. Aside from the least sandpiper, species were selected because of their reliance on beach habitats and their frequency of observation on Delaware Bay aerial surveys from 1986 to 2002 (see Clark et al. 1993; Table 5.4): semipalmated sandpiper (40%), ruddy turnstone (29%), red knot (17%), sanderling (6%), dunlin (6%), and long-/short-billed dowitcher (2%). The least sandpiper was chosen because of its contrasting us of marsh habitats, rather than beaches, which indicates less of a dietary reliance on horseshoe crab eggs. Long-billed dowitchers are only rarely observed on Delaware Bay beaches.

2.2. Conservation Status and Protection

The U. S. Shorebird Conservation Plan describes 6 factors of vulnerability (population trend, relative abundance, breeding threats, non-breeding threats, breeding distribution, and non-breeding distribution) that were used to determine the conservation concern of North American-breeding shorebird populations (Brown et al. 2001*). Combinations of these factors were used to designate the conservation concern of shorebird populations as: highly imperiled, high concern, moderate concern, low concern, or not at risk. This type of assessment was used by the U. S. Fish and Wildlife Service (2002*) to develop a Congressionally-mandated list of Birds of Conservation Concern. Of the 8 species mentioned in Section 2.1, the red knot, ruddy turnstone, and sanderling are listed as species of high conservation concern in the U. S. Shorebird Conservation Plan (Brown et al. 2001*), and the red knot and short-billed dowitcher (primarily due to central and western populations) are listed as Birds of Conservation Concern by the U. S. Fish and Wildlife Service (2002*).

All migrant species are protected in the U. S. under the statutes of the Migratory Bird Treaty Act, as amended, and are recognized in international agreements such as the Western Hemisphere Convention and the Convention on Arctic Flora and Fauna. Because of its value to birds, Delaware Bay has received international recognition as a Western Hemisphere Shorebird Reserve Network site of hemispheric importance (>500,000 shorebirds annually), a Wetland of International Importance under the Ramsar Convention (>1% of a flyway waterbird population), and an Important Bird Area of global significance (because of large aggregations).

2.3. Vulnerability of Long-distance Migrant Shorebirds and the Red Knot Focus

Piersma and Baker (2000) outlined several critical life history traits of migrant shorebirds that include: low productivity, long lifespan, trophic specialization, gregariousness, immunospecialization, sometimes strong sexual selection, long flights, metabolic adaptations for flight endurance, a precise annual cycle clock, orientation mechanisms, geographic bottlenecks (reliance on a small number of wintering and stopover sites), and reduced genetic variability. The red knot epitomizes these critical life history traits, and their trophic specialization on marine environments makes them vulnerable to perturbations to these habitats, particularly at geographic bottlenecks. Piersma and Baker (2000) suggested that populations of long-distance, long-hop migrant shorebirds, such as the red knot, are mainly constrained by access to high quality non-breeding habitats, a concept previously championed by Myers (1983).

Hitchcock and Gratto-Trevor (1997) modeled a local decline of semipalmated sandpipers and found that out of 5 variables (fecundity, adult survivorship, juvenile survivorship, delayed recruitment, and immigration), adult survivorship had the most significant influence on the population decline. Reductions in adult survival, through over-hunting and possibly stopover habitat change, are suggested to have caused the drastic decreases, and possible extinction, of Eskimo and slender-billed curlews (Gill et al. 1998, Gretton 1991). Piersma and Baker (2000) suggest that the probability of death by exhaustion or infection increases exponentially and reproduction decreases logarithmically as energy stores at stopover departure time and body mass on breeding ground arrival decrease. Because changes in population size are so sensitive to levels and variation in adult survival, conservation of high quality stopover and wintering sites is critical. Historical population bottlenecks may have caused the low genetic variability currently observed in some shorebird populations (Piersma and Baker 2000).

2.4. Red Knot Distribution

The red knot breeds in arctic regions of Siberia, Alaska, Canada, and Greenland and is the largest arctic-nesting sandpiper (i.e. in the genus *Calidris*) in North America. Three populations of red knots are found in North America: the subspecies *C. c. islandica* breeds in the northeastern high Canadian arctic and Greenland, migrates through Iceland, and winters in western Europe; *C. c. roselaari* likely breeds in Alaska and migrates along the Pacific coast and likely through interior North America; and *C. c. rufa* breeds in the central Canadian arctic and migrates primarily along the eastern coast of North America (Piersma and Davidson 1992). Most *rufa* individuals winter along the coasts of South America, and the largest number of individuals are found along the Chilean and Argentine shorelines of Tierra del Fuego (Morrison and Ross 1989a). Breeding origins of knots wintering in the southern U. S. and migrating through the interior of the continent are not completely known (Harrington 2001).

2.5. Red Knot Annual Cycle

Southward migration of adult red knots begins in mid-July when between 5,000–15,000 birds have been observed in James Bay, Canada (Morrison and Harrington 1992). Adult knots arrive on the Atlantic coast of North America from mid-July to early August. Juveniles depart later than adults and migrate through eastern North America from late August to mid-September. Concentrations of fall migrants are more disperse than during spring migration (see section 3.3). September aggregations of 1,800–12,000 knots have recently been reported along the coast of Georgia (Harrington and Winn 2001*). Knots banded in Georgia generally winter in Florida (likely *C. c. roselarii*), where the mean wintering population is about 6,300 ± 3, 400 (SD) individuals (Harrington et al. 1988). Individuals wintering in southwest Florida have high site fidelity (Below 2001*). *Rufa* knots depart the northeastern U. S. by late August and early

September to undertake a trans-Atlantic Ocean flight to arrive on the north coast of the Suriname, French Guiana, and Brazil. From there, they overfly central Brazil, stop briefly in the Pantanal (on the Rio Negro's salt lakes late September to early October), reach maximum abundance in Lagoa do Peixe in October, and arrive in Tierra del Fuego by early November. Northward migration in Argentina begins in mid-February and persists through early April. From mid-February to mid-March, 5,000–7,000 knots were present daily in Bahía de San Antonio Oeste, Argentina (González et al. 2001). Main passage through Lagoa do Peixe, Brazil, (used by about 7,000 knots) occurs from mid-April through the first week of May (Nascimento 2001*). Birds depart the Maranhão coast of northeastern Brazil, where >10,000 knots have been observed (Nascimento 2001*), during early to mid-May. April aggregations of ≥6,000 knots have been noted in South Carolina (Harrington and Winn 2001*) and peak counts of 7,710– 8,955 knots have been recorded on the outer coast of Virginia (Truitt et al. 2001*), where birds banded in Argentina (27 knots), Delaware Bay (27) and Brazil (4) were observed. Large numbers of birds (maximum counts range from 19,445 to 95,490 knots) arrive in Delaware Bay during the second week of May and usually depart by the end of May or early June. Passage flights of knots have been observed in James Bay, Canada, (but not landing) in late May and early June (Morrison and Harrington 1992). Knots arrive on their Southampton Island breeding grounds during the first 10 days of June (P. Smith, Canadian Wildlife Service, personal communication). Incubation is 21–22 days, and both parents incubate the 4-egg clutch (see Harrington 2001). Fledging period is estimated to be about 18 days (see Harrington 2001). Females may depart the breeding grounds before males (see Harrington 2001).

2.6. Distribution and Migration Routes of Other Species

2.6.1. Ruddy turnstone

A Holarctic species, 3 populations of ruddy turnstones breed in North America: *A. i. intepres* breeds in western and northern Alaska and winters on Pacific islands and the Pacific coast of North America, a disjunct population *A. i. intepres* breeds in the Canadian high arctic and winters in Europe, and *A. i. morinella* breeds in the central and low Canadian arctic, into northeastern Alaska, and migrates primarily along the eastern coast of North America, including through Delaware Bay (Nettleship 2000). Highly coastal in its habitats, *morinella* winters in the southern U. S., throughout the Caribbean, and along the northern and eastern coasts of South America south (a few) to Tierra del Fuego (Morrison and Ross 1989a). Turnstones wintering on the western coasts of Central and South America may be either *morinella* or *interpres* (Nettleship 2000). The greatest winter aggregations of *morinella* occur in northern South America (Morrison and Ross 1989a).

2.6.2. Sanderling

Breeding distribution of the sanderling is similar to that of the red knot, but no subspecies have been described (MacWhirter et al. 2002). The wintering distribution is much broader than the knot —sanderlings are found along the shorelines of every continent except Antarctica

(MacWhirter et al. 2002). Sanderlings nesting in the northeastern Canadian High arctic are thought to winter in Europe, and other birds breeding in the eastern arctic likely use eastern Atlantic and interior flyways (MacWhirter et al. 2002). The population passing through Delaware Bay probably winters in the southeastern U. S., Caribbean, and South America (Morrison et al. 2001). The greatest aggregations of wintering birds are found along the Pacific coast, rather than the Atlantic coast, of South America (Morrison and Ross 1989a).

2.6.3. Semipalmated sandpiper

The semipalmated sandpiper breeds throughout the well-vegetated tundra of arctic and sub-arctic regions of North America. Although populations have not differentiated to the point of subspecies recognition, a decreasing cline in body size occurs from east to west (Gratto-Trevor 1992). Semipalmated sandpipers that use Delaware Bay are thought to nest in the eastern Canadian arctic and use the Atlantic flyway to travel to wintering grounds along the Caribbean and Atlantic coasts of South America (Harrington and Morrison 1979). Winter aggregations are greatest along the northern coast of South America (Morrison and Ross 1989a).

2.6.4. Dunlin

The breeding distribution of the dunlin is one of the most cosmopolitan of all small sandpipers. Populations in North America have differentiated into 3 subspecies: *C. a. arcticola* breeds in northern Alaska and northwest Canada and winters in southeastern Asia, *C. a. pacifica* breeds in western Alaska and winters primarily along the west coast of North America, and *C. a. hudsonia*, which passes though Delaware Bay, breeds in the eastern and central Canadian arctic and winters on the Atlantic and Gulf of Mexico coasts (Warnock and Gill 1996). Few dunlins of any subspecies winter south of Mexico (Warnock and Gill 1996). More dunlins may be found in marshes than on beaches of Delaware Bay (Burger et al. 1997).

2.6.5. Short-billed dowitcher

The short-billed dowitcher is restricted to North America, where 3 recognizable subspecies occur: *L. g. griseus* breeds in eastern Canada and winters in Central and South America, *L. g. hendersoni* breeds in Central Canada west of Hudson Bay and winters in on the Atlantic and Gulf of Mexico coasts, and *L. g. caurinus* breeds in southern Alaska and winters along the Pacific coast from California to South America (Jehl et al. 2001). Short-billed dowitchers in Delaware Bay are likely *L. g. griseus*. More short-billed dowitchers might use Delaware Bay marshes than beaches (Burger et al. 1997).

2.6.6. Long-billed dowitcher

The long-billed dowitcher is monotypic throughout its range in northeastern Russia, Alaska, and northwestern Canada (Takekawa and Warnock 2000). Its breeding range is more northern than the congeneric short-billed and Asiatic dowitchers (*L. semipalmatus*). Long-billed dowitchers winter on the Pacific coast from southern British Columbia to El Salvador and eastward to North Carolina (Takekawa and Warnock 2000). Most spring dowitchers in Delaware Bay are short-billeds.

2.6.7. Least sandpiper

The least sandpiper has the broadest and most southern distribution of any *Calidris* sandpiper breeding in North America; their range stretches across the northern boreal and sub-arctic region from Newfoundland to western Alaska (Cooper 1994). Populations have not differentiated to the point of subspecies recognition, but birds using the Atlantic flyway, including Delaware Bay, likely breed in eastern Canada (Morrison et al. 2001) and winter in the southeastern U. S., Caribbean, and northern South America. Winter aggregations are greatest along the northern coast of South America (Morrison and Ross 1989a). Least sandpipers tend to use marshes, rather than shorelines, of Delaware Bay during spring migration and are not recorded in large numbers on aerial beach surveys (see Clark et al. 1993).

3.0. ABUNDANCE AND DISTRIBUTION OF HORSESHOE CRABS

The horseshoe crab ranges from the Yucatan Peninsula to Maine and is most abundant between Virginia and New Jersey (Shuster 1982). The Delaware Bay hosts the largest concentration of spawning horseshoe crabs worldwide (Shuster and Botton 1985). Within Delaware Bay, spawning horseshoe crabs have been reported from Woodland Beach to Cape Henelopen in Delaware and from Sea Breeze to Cape May in New Jersey (Smith et al. 2002b,c). Some spawning may occur farther up the estuary but is probably restricted by salinity and the increasing presence of salt marsh and peat banks (Shuster and Botton 1985). Botton et al. (1988) observed fewer spawning crabs in proximity of peat beds. Density of spawning crabs on beaches varies annually (Smith et al. 2002b), although beaches within the lower to middle portion of Delaware Bay tend to support the highest spawning concentrations.

The high concentration of breeding crabs may be attributable to the abundance of sheltered, coarse-grained, well-drained sandy beaches that are conducive to spawning and egg incubation. In addition, large intertidal flats adjoining, or in close proximity, to these beaches likely provide important nursery habitat. High, wide, low-tide terraces also dissipate wave energy and create narrow, steep beaches. Low wave energy associated with tidal creeks may explain why high concentrations of horseshoe crab spawning have been observed in sandy areas within tidal creeks. Botton et al. (1988) estimated that only 10% of the New Jersey shoreline in Delaware Bay provided optimal horseshoe crab spawning habitat. However, horseshoe crabs are opportunistic and use other habitats that are less conducive to egg survival. Shuster (1982) suggested that beach temperature, moisture level, and oxygen concentration affected horseshoe crab egg viability. Eggs remain in the sand for 2–4 weeks before hatch. Crabs have been known to spawn subtidally, but the extent to which this occurs is unknown (Atlantic States Marine Fisheries Commission 1998a*). Female crabs burrow into sediments to lay their eggs. Kraeuter and Fegley (1994) found that mean depth of sediment mixing (11 cm) corresponded closely to the mean carapace height of female crabs.

Mature horseshoe crabs move inshore from deeper portions of the bay and coastal waters in late spring to spawn (Atlantic States Marine Fisheries Commission 1998a*). Spawning in Delaware Bay may occur as early as April and last into July (Shuster and Botton 1985), with peak spawning activity typically occurring around the new and full moons in May or June. Spawning is usually higher on the highest of the 2 daily tides, which typically occur at night in Delaware Bay. Male horseshoe crabs often precede females to a beach and await the arrival of females (Shuster 1996). Maximum concentrations of spawning crabs may differ temporally between the New Jersey and Delaware sides of the Bay. For example, in 1999 maximum horseshoe crab spawning occurred in mid-May in New Jersey, but peaked in early June in Delaware (Smith et al. 2002c). Spawner abundance (adult females) during 1999–2000 was higher in Delaware than in New Jersey, but was higher in New Jersey in 2002 (Smith and Bennett 2003*). Previously, authors have reported higher spawning concentrations in New Jersey (Shuster and Botton 1985). Smith et al. (2002c) found that lunar phase (new/full) and wave height had the most significant effects on spawning activity, but effective modeling of spawning activity included a combination of time, place, weather, and tide height. In terms of an optimal design to survey spawning crabs, an increase in the number of sampled beaches had the greatest effect on reducing the CV (coefficient of variation) of the estimate of spawning females. Thus, spawning varied spatially and temporally and was moderated by wave height

Two years of Peterson disc tagging in Delaware Bay showed that horseshoe crabs spawn multiple times over a season, with males spawning more frequently than females, and that crabs appear to exhibit limited beach fidelity from year to year (Eyler and Millard 2002*). A combined acoustic and radio-tag study conducted by Brousseau et al. (2002*) also showed strong within-season fidelity to spawning beaches; 91% of the 23 crabs successfully tracked returned to spawn on beaches where they were initially tagged in the same year. Although sample sizes were low and observation duration was relatively short, the study also found that tagged female crabs remained between 50 and 250 m offshore from their known spawning beaches.

Besides providing food to shorebirds, horseshoe crab eggs and larvae are seasonal foods for fish [particularly striped bass (*Morone saxatilis*) and white perch (*Morone americana*)], crabs, and gastropods (Shuster 1982). Contributions of horseshoe crab eggs and larvae to the diet of these species is generally unknown (Atlantic States Marine Fisheries Commission 1998a*). Buckel and McKown (2002) found horseshoe crab eggs and juveniles in 42% of stomachs, which comprised 44% of identifiable prey items, of age 1 striped bass collected in beach seines in Long Island and Staten Island. Lutcavage and Musick (1985) determined that the most common prey of loggerhead turtles (*Caretta caretta*) in Chesapeake Bay were adult and sub-adult horseshoe crabs, which can represent ≥42% of the diet (Lutcavage 1981). Botton (1993) observed gulls feeding on live adult horseshoe crabs that were stranded on exposed beaches. Gulls attacked the exposed book-gills of overturned crabs. Through transect surveys, mortality was estimated at

7,760 crabs/km, and gull predation was suggested to be the most important source of mortality to crabs when they were exposed on spawning beaches.

4.0. POTENTIAL THREATS TO SHOREBIRDS

4.1. Heavy Metal Concentrations in Shorebirds and Horseshoe Crabs

Data from the 1990s indicated that the levels of metals in body feathers of 3 species of shorebirds from Delaware Bay were generally not high enough to directly affect birds themselves (Burger et al. 1993). However, mercury levels were relatively high (red knot = 1.1 ppm, sanderling = 2.8 ppm) and suggested a need for further monitoring. Burger et al. (2002b) examined the levels of arsenic, cadmium, chromium, lead, manganese, mercury and selenium in the eggs, leg muscle, and carapace musculature (hereafter called apodeme, the fleshy part of the carapace) in female horseshoe crabs from 4 beaches in New Jersey and 4 beaches in Delaware to determine whether there were location differences in metal levels, and whether these levels were high enough to cause effects in birds that eat them. If the crabs were obtaining heavy metals in the period immediately before egg laying, and sequestering them in their eggs, then the eggs from female crabs that nest farther north in the bay, where industrialization is greater, should have higher levels. Eggs were examined because they could be compared to levels reported earlier from the same study area (Burger 1997), and they are the major food resource for shorebirds migrating through the bay. Overall, there were some differences in metal levels of the crabs collected in New Jersey and Delaware, but the differences were generally not great and there was no consistent pattern in the bay. Previous work demonstrated horseshoe crab egg sensitivity to heavy metal toxicity (Botton et al. 1998, Botton 2000, Itow et al. 1998a, 1998b). Manganese concentrations in Delaware crabs (but not the eggs) were >2x than those from New Jersey. There were some location differences for all 3 tissues (except eggs in Delaware) for both New Jersey and Delaware. Although the differences were significant, they were generally not great; there were no order of magnitude differences among collection sites. Contaminant levels were generally low. The levels of contaminants found in horseshoe crabs were well below those known to cause adverse effects in the crabs themselves or in organisms that consume them or their eggs. Contaminant levels have generally declined in the eggs of horseshoe crabs from 1993–2000 in Delaware Bay, suggesting that contaminants are not likely to be a problem for secondary consumers. While it is important to examine the levels of metals in horseshoe crabs from Delaware Bay, it is equally important to understand contaminant patterns along the east coast of North America. This study is reported below.

Burger et al. (2002a) examined the levels of metals (arsenic, cadmium, chromium, lead, manganese, mercury, and selenium) in the eggs, leg muscle, and apodeme of 100 horseshoe crabs collected at 9 sites from Maine to Florida. Crabs were collected from the spawning beaches during 2000. Only large females (n = 5–16 per location) were collected to control for possible sexual differences and to increase the likelihood of obtaining egg samples. Arsenic levels were the highest, followed by manganese and selenium, and levels for the other metals averaged below 100 ppb for most tissues. Arsenic and mercury levels were highest in the leg muscle, cadmium, lead, manganese, and selenium levels were highest in eggs, and chromium levels were highest in the apodeme. There were significant geographical differences for all metals in all 3 tissues. No one geographical site had the highest levels of >2metals. Arsenic, with the highest levels overall, was highest in Florida in all 3 tissues. Manganese levels were highest in Massachusetts for eggs and apodeme, but not leg, which was highest in Port Jefferson, New York. Selenium was highest in apodeme from Florida, and in eggs and leg muscle from Prime Hook, Delaware. The patterns among locations and tissues were not as clear for the other metals because the levels generally averaged below 100 ppb. The levels of contaminants found in horseshoe crabs, with the possible exception of arsenic in Florida, and mercury from Barnegat Bay and Prime Hook, were below those known to cause adverse effects in the crabs themselves, or in organisms that consume them or their eggs, even in relatively large quantities. These results indicate that site-specific data are essential for managers to evaluate the potential threat from contaminants to both the horseshoe crabs and to their consumers.

4.2. Organic Compound Concentrations in Shorebirds and Horseshoe Crabs

Maghini (1996*) collected sand, horseshoe crab eggs, and ruddy turnstones, at 2 locations, Port Mahon and South Bower Beach, along the Delaware shoreline. Sites were selected to sample resident and migrant horseshoe crab populations, which could be exposed to different contaminant sources. Sediment and egg samples at each site were collected 1–4 June 1992 along 10 (non-randomly selected) transects located perpendicular to the shoreline. Sand within 25 cm of the surface was collected at 10 stations along each transect. Horseshoe crab eggs were also collected along the 10 transects. Twenty-two turnstones were shot at Port Mahon, and none were collected from South Bower Beach. Chemical analyses were conducted by the Geochemical Environmental Research Group at Texas A&M University. Quality assurance measures were conducted by the laboratory and considered satisfactory. Many samples had concentrations of organic compounds that were below the limits of detectability. Maghini (1996*) found that concentrations of DDE and PCBs in turnstones were at background concentrations, but 2 carcasses had concentrations of DDT that suggested recent exposure. Although concentrations of lead, mercury, and cadmium were detectable in sand and tissue samples, most were within background concentrations. Arsenic and selenium concentrations were elevated in turnstone tissues, but were similar to other species that fed on marine invertebrates and fish. Similar concentrations in horseshoe crab eggs suggest that they were the likely route of exposure. Conclusions were that concentrations of trace metals and organochlorines presented low toxicological risk. However, wider geographic and taxonomic sampling, component analysis of arsenic in eggs, and measurement of selenium concentrations in livers of turnstones were suggested. Little is known about chemical concentrations in shorebird wintering areas.

4.3. Disease in Shorebirds

Piersma (1997) suggested that shorebirds may make a trade-off between investments in immunofunctioning and growth (chicks) or sustained exercise. Some shorebird species appear to be restricted to parasite-poor habitats (seashores, the arctic). Red knot chicks raised in the high arctic had daily energy expenditures that were 1.5x higher than temperate shorebirds of the same mass, yet grew at a faster rate. For migrant birds, optimal areas are separated seasonally by long-distances. If long-distance shorebirds are adapted to use parasite-poor habitats, they may be particularly susceptible to parasites and pathogens. Captive red knots only remained healthy after sea water was flushed through their holding cages, which suggested that they may be particularly susceptible to common avian pathogens. Figuerola (1999) found that haematoza infection rates in waterbirds, when controlling for phylogeny and population size, were greater in freshwater species than in those inhabiting saline habitats. Low reproductive success could be a cost associated with breeding in the climatically-marginal, but parasite-low, arctic. Increased adult survival afforded by inhabiting areas of low parasite loads may offset these costs.

The Southeastern Cooperative Wildlife Disease Study (2002*) sampled 905 shorebirds from Delaware beaches in 2000 and 501 shorebirds (and 75 fecal samples) in 2001 for occurrence of influenza viruses. Virus was isolated from 5 species. The ruddy turnstone ($n = 368$) had the highest incidence rate (>13%), and lesser incidence rates (<5%) were found in red knots ($n = 620$), dunlins ($n = 164$), semipalmated sandpipers ($n = 107$), and short-billed dowitchers ($n = 68$). Fecal samples collected off the ground in areas of turnstone activity revealed isolation of 5 viruses. Preliminary results from 2002 were similar. One interesting note is that a turnstone in Delaware Bay that did not have the virus on 21 May tested positive when it was recaptured on 28 May.

In 1997, dead and dying red knots (46), white-rumped sandpipers (11), and sanderlings (3) were discovered in the area of Lagoa do Peixe, Brazil (Baker et al. 1998). All of the 35 collected knots were infected by hookworms (*Acanthocephala* spp.). About 150 knots found sick or dead in western Florida had their digestive tract infected by an unidentified sporozoan-type protozoan parasite (Woodward et al. 1977). Although no dramatic die-offs have been observed over the last 2 decades, information on parasite loads of Delaware Bay's shorebirds is lacking and should be evaluated. Following Piersma's (1997) hypothesis, Delaware Bay beaches could provide important, low-parasite environments needed by foraging red knots.

4.4. Shoreline Changes in Delaware Bay

Shoreline habitat change can reduce horseshoe crab spawning habitat and consequently shorebird feeding habitat. Residential development along Delaware Bay's beachfront can have negative, direct and indirect, effects on foraging and roosting shorebirds. Storm damage and longshore transport of sand can greatly affect beach characteristics. Bulkheads may block access to intertidal spawning beaches, and seawalls and groins can intensify local shoreline erosion and prevent natural beach migration (Atlantic States Marine Fisheries Commission 1998a*). Over the last 100 years, beaches in New Jersey have eroded at a rate of 0.3–3.7 m/year and in Delaware at a rate of 0.3–7.9 m/year (mean = 0.9–1.5 m/year, U. S. Army Corps of Engineers 1991*, 1997*), and are presently at 2–6 m/year (Galofre 2002*). Increased turbidity, siltation, and peat exposure caused by erosion creates anaerobic conditions in horseshoe crab nests and reduces egg survivorship (Botton et al. 1988). Few crabs tend to spawn on beaches with much peat. Natural and human creation of inlets (e.g., Thompson's and Moore's Beaches) may have channeled crabs into marshes where they were harvested or failed to successfully reproduce (see <www.delawarebay.com>). Sand nourishment on beaches can increase habitat for spawning horseshoe crabs if sediment types match natural beaches favorable to breeding horseshoe crabs (see section 7.6). Monitoring and management of beach conditions will likely be needed to sustain habitats for spawning crabs and foraging shorebirds.

4.5. Sea Level Rise from Global Climate Change

Galbraith et al. (2002) used U. S. Environmental Protection Agency data on historical sea level rise to predict sea level change at sites important to shorebirds. Assuming global temperature changes of 2°C (50% chance) or 4.7°C (5%), resultant sea level rise would be 0.34 m (50% chance) or 0.77 m (5%). Local rates of historical sea level change were used with the Sea Level Affecting Marshes Model (SLAMM 4) to predict local effects of sea level rise by 2100. Based on historical rates, sea level in Delaware Bay would rise 0.3 m by 2100, with a 50% chance of rising 0.6 m. With these rates of sea level rise, tidal flats in Delaware Bay would decrease by 23% under a historical rise and a predicted 50% chance of a 57% loss. A corresponding increase in salt marsh ($\approx$ 10%) would occur. These estimates do not account for any mitigation measures undertaken (e.g., seawalls). If losses of this magnitude occurred, Delaware Bay might not be able to support historical levels of shorebird use. Increased "storminess" associated with global climate change could further alter Delaware Bay's shoreline habitats.

4.6. Arctic Breeding Ground Conditions

Reproduction in arctic-breeding birds is known to be highly variable. Inter-annual variability in the reproductive success of shorebirds is usually attributed to weather or predation. Variability in predation on shorebird nests has been suggested as an indirect consequence of the cyclical abundance of lemmings. When lemmings are abundant, predators primarily rely on them as food; when lemmings are scarce, predators switch to other sources like birds. Blomqvist et al. (2002) used a 50-year series of fall banding data of red knots (*C. c. canutus*) migrating through the Baltic Sea in southern Sweden (Ottenby), and other information in the literature, to test the "bird-lemming hypothesis". They predicted that: 1) juvenile red knot numbers would correlate with lemming fluctuations, 2) adult red knot numbers would not correlate with lemming numbers, and 3) post-breeding migration of adults would be earlier in years of high predation pressure. As an alternative hypothesis, they examined the correlation of climatic oscillations and breeding success.

At Ottenby, Blomqvist et al. (2002) found no significant ($P > 0.05$) long-term trend in the number of adult or juvenile knots and no significant correlation between the annual numbers of adults and juveniles. Predation index from the Taimyr region of Russia was significantly and negatively associated with median knot passage date at Ottenby; proportional den use by foxes correlated with lemming abundance in arctic Russia. Predation index was significantly and negatively correlated with the number of juvenile knots captured at Ottenby, but not with the number of captured adults. Numbers of juveniles captured at banding stations in South Africa and Germany were also negatively associated with the predation index. Fourier analysis of the time series of juvenile captures revealed a periodicity of 3 years, which matched the median date of adult passage and lemming abundance in the Russian arctic. May weather did not correlate with any shorebird population variables. Blomqvist et al. (2002) found that patterns in Swedish knots were similar for curlew sandpiper (*Calidris ferruginea*) and likely extend to numerous other arctic-breeding species (see Underhill et al. 1993). Productivity of red knots and other shorebirds on eastern Southampton Island appears to be similarly correlated to abundance to of lemmings (P. Smith, Canadian Wildlife Service, unpublished data).

Zöckler and Lysenko (2000) used a climate change model (HadCM2GSal), with a 1% increase of CO_2/year, and Dynamic General Vegetation Models to examine effects of climate change on Holarctic waterbird populations. Of all biomes, tundra areas are expected to suffer the greatest climate-related habitat change. Major habitat changes for *Calidris* sandpipers, particularly in the low Canadian arctic, are predicted. Southampton Island is predicted to undergo major tundra loss, while part of northeastern Canada and Greenland are predicted to cool. Habitat changes have not yet occurred, but temperature changes are underway. Temperatures have risen by $1.3°C$ over the last 30 year at Resolute, Canada (Falkingham et al. 2001*). Mean July temperature in breeding areas was positively, but not significantly, correlated ($r = 0.3$) with the percentage of juvenile *islandica* red knots observed in the subsequent season on wintering grounds. Boyd (1992), however, suggested that a relationship existed between mean June temperature in northeastern Canadian arctic and the total number of knots observed in Great Britain the subsequent winter. More recently, Boyd and Piersma (2001) found that cold arctic summers affected both productivity and adult survival of knots wintering in Britain.

Little information exists on the biology or productivity of *rufa* red knots on their breeding grounds. Knots (20 of 165) radio-tagged in Delaware Bay were relocated on breeding grounds on Southampton and Prince William Islands, Canada (Niles et al. 2001*). Knots tended to use low elevation, barren tundra located within 50 km of the coast. Eleven nests in sparsely vegetated tundra (e.g., eskers, frost boils), often associated with *Dryas*, were found in 2000. Topographical placement of nests may depend on the amount of snow cover when birds arrive, but nests are usually located ≤180 m of isolated wetlands. Nest density on Southampton Island ranged from 0.85 nests/km^2 in 2000 to 0.58 nests/km^2 in 2002 (Niles et al. 2003*). No dramatic weather events occurred on Southampton Island during the breeding seasons of 1999–2002 (L. Niles, personal communication).

4.7. South American Wintering Ground Conditions

In general, much of the Patagonia and Tierra del Fuego coast line is in good ecological condition (see descriptions at <http://www.ramsar.org> and <http://www.whsrn.org>). However, oil exploration and its associated infrastructure pose risks for migrant shorebirds that depend on intertidal feeding areas. Some wells have been placed in intertidal areas and development of oil industry infrastructure has lead to water and wind erosion of beach environments. Spills from oil storage and transfer facilities and oil tankers' illegal ballast discharges are probably the greatest threat to migrant and wintering shorebirds. Although the region is still sparsely populated, much of the human population in concentrated in coastal areas, and pollution from untreated sewage is increasing and may have a future, negative effect on shorebirds. Season tourism brings needed cash to the region, but recreational beach activities (walking, shellfish collecting, vehicles, dogs) can disturb feeding and roosting shorebirds. Negative human disturbance effects are often greatest near cities. Installation of an ash plant (for the production of glass) could negatively affect shorebirds that use Bahía San Antonio Oeste. The plant could release ≥250,000 tons of calcium chloride into the bay annually, that could destroy the clams, mussels, oysters and other food sources upon which migrating shorebirds depend. Lagoa do Peixe is a large, shallow coastal lagoon in southern Brazil that has a highly variable, natural hydrology. Depending on rainfall and winds, the lagoon can dry up completely during the austral summer. Thus, shorebird use can be highly variable among years. Further north along the Maranhão coast of Brazil, shrimp farming could alter coastal systems in a way that is detrimental to migrant shorebirds. Despite potential threats, the southern wintering grounds of red knots do not appear to have changed dramatically in the last decade.

4.8. Human Disturbance to Shorebirds

Nesting and migrant shorebirds are susceptible to disturbance caused by human activities. Human disturbance can force shorebirds to: 1) shift to feeding areas with fewer numbers of humans (Burger and Gochfeld 1991), 2) entirely abandon an area (Pfister et al. 1992, Smit and Visser 1993), or 3) increase vigilance, movement, or escape flights (flushing). Disturbance can therefore reduce feeding time and increase energy requirements at a time when migrant birds need fuel for migration (Hockin et al. 1992, Davidson and Rothwell 1993, Lafferty 2001). Distance to birds was the best measure of disruption to foraging sanderlings on California beaches (Thomas et al. 2003). Free-ranging dogs also disrupted foraging behavior and birds were completely excluded from beaches with intense vehicular use. The chronic disturbance of shorebirds can disrupt their behavior and cause them to use the energy they are trying to store for migration in an escape flight, thus affecting their energy balance and potentially their survival (Helmers 1992, Hockin et al. 1992, Davidson and Rothwell 1993, Harrington and Drilling 1996, Brown et al. 2001*, Gill et al. 2001, Lafferty 2001, West et al. 2002).
Disturbance, frequently measured by flushing rate, has a greater effect on migratory bird species than on resident species (Burger and Gochfeld 1991). Anecdotal observations of shorebird researchers in Delaware (Carter et al. 2002*) and numerous published studies have noted negative human disturbance effects on shorebirds caused by: 1) walking and jogging (Burger 1981), 2) windsurfing and hunting (Madsen 1998), 3) dog-walking, bird-watching, and shell-fishing (Goss-Custard and Verboven 1993), 4) automobiles, boats and all-terrain vehicles (Rodgers and Smith 1997), 5) personal watercraft and outboard-powered boats (Rodgers and Schwikert 2002), and 6) aircraft (Koolhaas et al. 1993). Flushing distances have been shown to vary between types of disturbance, individual birds, and species. Researchers associated with national and regional shorebird conservation plans identified the high priority need to gain more

information on how human disturbance affects shorebirds (Clark and Niles 2000*, Oring et al. 2000*).

Although no specific studies have been conducted to quantify disturbance effects to shorebirds in Delaware Bay, repeated disturbance along its beaches likely reduces shorebird feeding efficiency thereby increasing energy expenditure and reducing energy intake. Efforts to reduce and minimize human disturbance from recreational and commercial activities, and from research studies, in Delaware Bay are ongoing. New Jersey has implemented regulations which reduce the potential for disturbance associated with the horseshoe crab fishery by curtailing the hand harvest from its beaches. Bird observation platforms in New Jersey and Delaware have been built to allow for viewing of shorebirds with minimal disturbance. Actions have also been adopted to minimize any potential disturbance impacts of research associated with the catching and observing of shorebirds.

4.9. Effect of Disturbance on Survival of Semipalmated Sandpipers

Pfister et al. (1998) present one of the few studies of a migratory species that demonstrates a relationship between body mass and annual return rate to a site of a migratory species. Semipalmated sandpipers were captured, color-marked, and measured during fall migration at Plymouth Beach. Massachusetts, in 1985 and 1986. Beaches was surveyed extensively during those 2 years for banded birds to determine the minimum length of stay for individuals. From Plymouth beach, semipalmated sandpipers are thought to make over-water crossings of >3,000 km. Using body fat estimates, length of stay, and a linear regression model derived from sandpiper banding and recapture data at this site during the 15 years from 1971 to 1984, the authors calculated percent body fat of 255 individual sandpipers departing from the site. During 1986 and 1987 surveys were conducted to determine how many birds banded the previous year returned to the site. A logistic regression model was used to relate return to the staging site (1 = return, 0 = no return) to the estimated fat levels at departure. Because of possible biases in the methods used to estimate fat at departure, an alternate method was also used to test the hypothesis that return rates are associated with fat levels. In this method, the authors used the difference between of actual length of stay and the time in days that would be needed to attain 40% body fat (based on linear regression of fat deposition rates from previously collected data) as an index of the likelihood that birds would attain the desirable departure weight before migration. Birds were separated into 3 risk groups based on how many days short they were of attaining that level of 40% body fat. In both the estimated fat levels at departure and the risk of not attaining favorable fat levels at departure models, regression analysis revealed that fat level at departure had a significant association with return rate. The authors suggest that the association between fat levels and annual return rate is due to differences in return rates caused by fat depletion during the non-stop flight over water. The results support the idea that disturbance reducing the feeding efficiency of shorebirds at staging areas can reduce the ability of these migrants to attain high fat levels for their migratory flights and therefore may lead to their mortality.

4.10. Horseshoe Crab Bait Landings

The Atlantic States Marine Fisheries Commission adopted a Fishery Management Plan for Horseshoe Crab in 1998. It limited landings in New Jersey, Delaware, and Maryland (in recognition of that these states had already acted to reduce harvest levels) to existing harvest levels, encouraged other states to reduce harvest, and recommended development of a coast-wide cap on commercial bait landings in 2000. Adopted in 2000, Addendum 1 established landings for the 1995–1997 reference period and state-specific 25% reductions in 2000 landings from the reference period (Atlantic States Marine Fisheries Commission 2000*). It was recognized that some states had already reduced harvest >25% below the reference period, and these states were encouraged to maintain their current reductions (about 211,000 crabs in Maryland and 297,680 crabs in New Jersey). States that harvested <1% of the coast-wide landings were exempted from the 25% reduction (reviewed annually). In addition, Addendum 1 asked the National Marine Fisheries Service to establish a horseshoe crab sanctuary at the mouth of Delaware Bay. In 2001, the sanctuary was established and now protects 3,885 km^2 of crab habitat from harvest. Also in 2001, Addendum II of the fishery management plan was adopted to establish procedures for inter-state transfer of harvest quotas (Atlantic States Marine Fisheries Commission 2001*). After adoption of Addendum I in 2000, coast-wide reductions in crab bait landings ranged from 37 to 58%, and bait landings were reduced 34–75% in New Jersey, Delaware, and Maryland (Table 4.1). Some unknown portion of crabs that breed in Delaware Bay are likely landed in Maryland. Because horseshoe crabs have a delayed sexual maturity of about 9 years, changes in population size that resulted from increased harvest in the mid-1990s and subsequent restrictions not yet been realized.

4.11. Changes in Horseshoe Crab Populations

The Atlantic States Marine Fisheries Commission Horseshoe Crab Stock Assessment Sub-committee (Millard et al. 2000*) recommended that 3 surveys, as interim measures until a stock assessment is completed (Atlantic States Marine Fisheries Commission 1998b*,c*), be evaluated to determine short-term trends of horseshoe crab populations: 1) re-designed Delaware Bay spawning survey, 2) Delaware trawl survey, and 3) National Marine Fisheries Service fall trawl survey.

The Delaware Bay Horseshoe Crab Spawning Survey was substantially modified in 1999 to provide a statistically reliable survey of spawning crabs. In 2002, volunteers conducted 243 tide-based surveys on 23 beaches of New Jersey (10 beaches) and Delaware (13 beaches). An index of spawning activity is calculated as the number of spawning females within 1 m of high tide on beach index sites. Smith et al. (2002c) recommended that females be used to assess spawning activity because: 1) female abundance is the most direct measure of reproductive potential, 2) distribution of females is less variable than males, and 3) counting females alone is more cost-effective. In 2002, spawning, which peaked in late May, tended to be somewhat higher in New Jersey than in Delaware (Smith and Bennett 2003*). Since 1999, spawning activity has remained unchanged in New Jersey (slope = 0.06, SE = 0.04, P = 0.29) and in Delaware (slope =

-0.08, SE = 0.03, P = 0.16). Substantial shifts in spawning concentrations were noted from previous years. In 2002, for example, there were large increase in spawning activity on New Jersey beaches in the upper bay. Increases on some New Jersey beaches may or may not compensate for declines elsewhere. However, bay-wide spawning activity has been stable over the past 4 years, indicating some degree of compensation. Smith et al. (2002c) found that the number of sampled beaches and temporal stratification were the most important determinants of achieving the power needed to detect changes in spawning activity.

The Delaware 30-foot trawl survey has been conducted consistently between March and December since 1990; horseshoe crab information is restricted to the April–July period. The State of Delaware has also conducted a 16-foot trawl survey, for the last 11 years, that targets juvenile (<160 mm wide) and young-of-the-year crabs. The National Marine Fisheries Service (NMFS; 2002*) has conducted a fall trawl survey along the Atlantic coast since 1977. Horseshoe crab information was restricted to the region between New York and Cape Hatteras, and only stations $\leq$27 m deep were used to calculate crab abundances. Gear for the NMFS survey changed dramatically over the course of a few years in the mid-1980s and invalidated analysis of the complete time series. Geometric means of annual all crab catches in the 30-foot trawl have decreased since 1990 (linear regression, R^2 = 0.661, P = 0.0007; S. Michels, unpublished data). Although counts in most recent years appear to be stable, the lowest recorded catch in 13 years occurred in 2002 (Figure 1). Also, mean catch per unit effort was significantly (P <0.025) lower in later years of the survey relative to the early 1990s (Table 4.2; Andres analysis). Although not significant, differences between periods were in the same direction as the 30-foot trawl survey for juvenile and young-of-the-year crabs in the 16-foot trawl and for all crabs caught in the NMFS fall survey (Table 4.2; Andres analysis; Figure 2,3). Note that the catch per unit effort for these latter surveys is very low. Horseshoe crab populations may now be stable but are likely at lower levels than in the early 1990s, and possible decreases may be apparent in all age classes of the population. Preliminary estimates from trawl surveys off of Delaware Bay (extending approximately from Ocean City, Maryland, to Atlantic City, New Jersey, and 22.2 km offshore) indicate a total population of 11,400,000 ± 5,453,000 crabs (95% confidence interval), of which about 2.7 million are spawning age females (Berkson and Hata, unpublished data). The estimate of primiparus females ranges from 200,000 to 522,000 crabs. This does not include any animals within the Delaware Bay or animals beyond 22.2 km, assumes 100% gear efficiency, and should therefore be considered a minimal estimate. Landings of female horseshoe crabs for the states of Delaware, Maryland, and New Jersey in 2002 totaled 297,932 crabs, suggesting that the stock may be rebuilding as recruitment is exceeding landings in this area (but the 95% confidence limit of the estimate includes the landings value).

5.0. ESTIMATES OF SHOREBIRD POPULATION SIZES AND TRENDS

5.1. Shorebird Population Sizes

5.1.1. Coarse continental estimates

Morrison et al. (2001) compiled published and unpublished counts of shorebirds, by season and region, to generate coarse, flyway population estimates for North American-breeding shorebirds. They used the maximum summation of counts within a region to determine population size. For example, maximum counts of red knots at all sites on the Atlantic coast, during northward migration, would be summed to produce an estimate of that flyway's population. All regions would then be summed to produce a continental estimate. These estimates were thought to be the minimum population present during the late 1980s and early 1990s. The method would likely only over-estimate population size, by counting individuals multiple times, if large numbers of the same individuals would stop at a few sites within the same region. Each estimate was assigned an accuracy (confidence) score which reflected quality and breadth of data used to generate the estimate. Of the 8 species considered in this report, populations in eastern North America range from 11,300 to 994,600 individuals (Table 5.1). Confidence in estimates for these species ranged from low to moderate. The population of *rufa* red knots was estimated to be 170,000 (150,000 birds in eastern North America) in the late 1980s and was one of the smallest populations of red knots known to occur throughout the world (Piersma and Davidson 1992).

5.1.2. Re-sighting banded red knots in the 1980s

Between 1980 and 1987, Harrington (2002*) and his colleagues marked red knots with color bands in North and South America. Between springs of 1981 and 1990, Delaware Bay knots were scanned for color bands. This information allowed for calculation of the frequency with which birds of each band cohort (a group of birds banded at the same location in the same year) were found. This number, in combination with an estimate of annual survivorship of knots and known band cohort sizes, was used to estimate the population size as: [(number checked for bands*estimated number alive) ÷ number of cohort birds found]. The estimated number alive is the [(cohort size*(monthly survival rate* number of months since banding)]. The re-sighting rate was calculated as: {[(number of cohort-marked birds found ÷ expected cohort number alive) ÷ number of birds checked for bands]*1000}. The expected cohort number alive was the original number banded in the cohort reduced to adjust for an annual survivorship of 0.752 (details on model selection are not provided). A population estimate of red knots (*rufa*) made for each year was based on band re-sighting ratios of knots banded in Massachusetts during fall and re-sighted in New Jersey in spring, and on knots banded in New Jersey in spring and re-sighted in New Jersey in spring. Before estimates were calculated, cohorts were removed if <5 banded birds from a cohort were observed per 1,000 birds checked . This removed re-sighted cohorts where the original banding cohort was small. In addition, 2 cohorts were removed (banded on Delaware Bay in 1980 and 1981) where color band loss was a problem. Mean re-sighting rates of knots banded in Massachusetts and re-sighted in New Jersey were compared to that of birds both banded and re-sighted in New Jersey. The 2 groups were not significantly different (F-test, $P > 0.05$) and were therefore combined. Separate population estimates were calculated for each band cohort during each re-sighting year. For example, estimates, adjusted for survivorship, were made for a cohort banded in Massachusetts in 1984 and re-sighted in New Jersey 10, 22, 34, 46, 58, and 70 months later.

Annual population size estimates during 9 years between 1981 and 1990 ranged from $59,215 \pm 16,085$ (1990) to $212,885 \pm 49,575$ (1981). Ranges of the annual standard deviations of these estimates was 20–40% of their corresponding annual population estimate (Table 5.2) The overall mean of 28 separate estimates was $143,680 \pm 13,579$ (SE). There was no population trend evident among the yearly estimates ($R^2 = 0.003$, $P = 0.74$). Note, however, that little is known of the size and annual variation of the non-breeding (presumably sub-adult) population, which evidently remains in South America and the southeastern U. S. during the northern summer. Some unknown portion of sub-adults visit Delaware Bay each spring. Finally, little is known of how the size of the non-breeding population relates to the size of the breeding population or to annual variation of breeding production. The mean re-sighting estimate of population size of knots in eastern North America in the 1980s was similar to the coarse estimate (see Table 5.1) generated by Morrison et al. (2001).

5.1.3. Red knot band re-sighting in South America

González et al. (2001*) color-banded 107 red knots in Rio Grande, Tierra del Fuego, Argentina, in December 2000 and used re-sighting information from there and Bahia de San Antonio (1,450 km to the north), in early 2001, to estimate the population size of red knots wintering in southern South America. Scans of Rio Grande-banded birds re-sighted at San Antonio gave an estimate of the entire population wintering south of San Antonio stopover (in Rio Grande and Bahía Lomas) as 31,800 (95% confidence interval = 26,850–37,850). Scans of San Antonio-banded birds re-sighted at either site gave an estimate of 37,600 individuals, which was likely an estimate of the southern South American wintering population. This estimate corresponds fairly well with estimates from aerial surveys made during the same period (see section 5.2.1). If the current population of knots wintering in southern South America is about 30,000 individuals, and the population wintering in northern South America is about 15,000 birds (A. J. Baker, personal communication), then the total population of *rufa* red knots ($\approx$ 45,000 birds) is probably substantially lower than late 1980s levels. Maximum counts on spring aerial surveys in Delaware Bay (see section 5.2.2) from 2000–2002 were lower than this estimated value (Table 5.4).

5.2. Shorebird Population Trends

5.2.1. Aerial surveys of red knots in South America

Aerial surveys, usually with fixed-winged aircraft, were conducted along the southern South America coastline during the boreal winter 1982–86 (Morrison and Ross 1989a,b). The

Argentine coast was surveyed in 1982 and Tierra del Fuego was flown in 1985. Flights, at high tide when possible, were made at an altitude of 50–80 m and 160 km/hour. The flight line was selected to survey the most important marine-influenced habitats and was usually 50 m offshore. Shorebirds were identified to species (except for small *Calidris* sandpipers) unless conditions or size of flocks prevented a reasonable assessment. Along the Atlantic coast of South America, red knots ($n = 76,392$ birds) were distributed among Tierra del Fuego (69.7%), the Argentine Patagonian coast (18.7%), northern Brazil (10.9%), and western Venezuela (0.7%). In Tierra del Fuego, the most important site was Bahia Lomas where 41,700 knots were counted (54.6% of all observations). Aerial surveys of the same shorelines of Tierra del Fuego were repeated with the same methods and same observers in 2000–2002. Counts of red knots made in Bahia Lomas, and for the entirety of Tierra del Fuego, in 2000 tended to be similar to counts made in 1982/85 (Table 5.3). However, substantial decreases in knot counts, relative to 2000, occurred in 2001 and 2002 (Table 5.3). A complete survey of Tierra del Fuego and the Patagonia coast in 2002 indicated that knots did not re-distribute themselves at sites north of Tierra del Fuego (Table 5.3). Numbers from Tierra del Fuego in 2003, although analysis is incomplete, suggest a slight increase from 2002 levels (R. I. G. Morrison, personal communication). Lack of a longer time series precludes a thorough analysis of this dataset. Ground counts and re-sighting information suggests that knot numbers at San Antonio declined from >20,000 in 1996 to 15,000 in 1997–1998 and further to 8,500 (±500) in 2001. Because of relative stability on wintering grounds, continued surveys of southern South America could provide important information on knot population change.

5.2.2. Spring aerial surveys in Delaware Bay

To determine shorebird use in Delaware Bay, weekly aerial surveys of the entire shoreline of Delaware Bay have been conducted, since 1986, by 2 constant observers, and 1 recorder, in a Cessna 172 (see Clark et al. 1993). Flights, at a height of 30 m above the shoreline, started at Cape May 3 hours after high tide, headed north along the New Jersey coast to the mouth of the Delaware River, and then turned south along Delaware's shoreline to end at Cape Henlopen. Because little information exists on species-specific turnover rates, the maximum counts obtained during a single flight are used to determine changes in numbers in Delaware Bay. Yearly maximum counts are provided in Table 5.4. Using this method, Niles et al. (2003*) found that the maximum annual counts of red knots differed among recent years (1998–2002; Kruskal-Wallis, $\chi^2 = 19.26$, df = 5, $P = 0.002$). A decrease in maximum red knot counts was marginally significant ($P = 0.068$) from 1997 to 2002 (Andres analysis; Kendall's nonparametric concordance test; Hollander and Wolfe 1973:185–199). The mean of maximum knot counts, however, did not differ between 1986–1996 and 1997–2002 periods (Table 5.5). No other species showed consistent declines, but maximum counts of dunlins and dowitchers have increased significantly in recent years (Table 5.5). Because of their unknown relationship to real population size, maximum aerial survey counts are not be useful to determine population change.

5.2.3. International and Maritime Shorebird Surveys

Bart et al. (2003*) used data from the Maritime Shorebird Survey (MSS) and the complementary International Shorebird Survey (ISS) data to assess trends in migrant shorebird numbers along the north Atlantic coast (from Georgia to Newfoundland). The primary purpose of these surveys is to document abundance and distribution of migrant shorebirds. Volunteers visit sites every 10–14 days, when shorebirds are present in the site's region, and count all shorebirds. ISS guidelines ask that counts (or estimates) of all shorebird species be made once each third month (once between the 1st and 10th, once between the 11th and 20th, and once after the 20th) during spring (1 April–10 June) and fall (10 July–31 October) migration. Migration periods were defined for each species by determining the 20th and 80th percentiles of the cumulative distribution of spring and fall periods. A linear model was used to determine site-specific rates of change in shorebird numbers, for sites that had >3 visits, and were combined to determine an average rate of change. Only species that were observed at ≥ 8 sites were included in the analysis, and highly significant outliers (residual $P < 0.005$) were removed from the analysis. Morrison and Hicklin (2001*) independently used average counts at "paired" Canadian Maritime sites to make comparisons between decades (1970s, 1980s, and 1990s). They reported the sign of the difference (negative or positive) and the significance (P-value) of the difference. Bart et al. (2003*) found that knot counts declined, but not significantly ($P > 0.1$), at a rate of 1.65%/year in eastern North America. Sanderling, semipalmated sandpiper, and least sandpiper all decreased at significant rates (≈ 4–7%, $P < 0.05$) in the ISS/MSS analysis (Table 5.6). Red knots and semipalmated sandpipers were the only species that showed consistent, negatives changes among time periods and analysis methods (Table 5.6). In a previous analysis of ISS data, sanderlings had decreased substantially (Howe et al. 1989). P. Hicklin (unpublished data) has found a shift in the distribution of bill lengths of semipalmated sandpipers captured while migrating through the Bay of Fundy, Canada. Proportionally fewer long-billed birds, those from the most eastern population that use Delaware Bay in the spring, have been captured in recent years.

5.2.4. Quebec migration checklists

Since 1950, opportunistic information has been collected from daily checklists of volunteer birders in Quebec. These records have been computerized and were used by Aubry and Cotter (2001*) to assess the population trends of fall-migrating shorebirds in the province. They used the frequency of occurrence of shorebird species occurrence on checklists, from 1976 to 1998, to determine if reporting rates changed through time. From this analysis, significant decreases were found in reporting frequencies for ruddy turnstones, red knots, and semipalmated sandpipers (Table 5.6). Decreases in the latter 2 species are consistent with ISS/MSS analyses.

6.0. IMPORTANCE OF DELAWARE BAY TO SHOREBIRD POPULATIONS

Harrington (2002*) compared 8 years of population estimates of red knots in the in the 1980s (see section 5.1.2) to aerial surveys conducted during the same period (see section 5.2.2). A consistent relationship between the maximum count and the population size would only exist if a constant proportion of the spring migrating knot population uses Delaware Bay each year. No significant relationship ($\square$ 0.27, $P = 0.51$) existed between annual estimates of population size determined from color-banding ratios and maximum counts from annual spring aerial surveys. On average, the maximum aerial survey count represented 38% of the adult population size estimates from the same 8 years and ranged from 14 to 77%. Therefore, Delaware Bay is likely not used by a consistent proportion of the knots each year, and use varies considerably among years. Note that the error for population estimates is relatively high (see Table 5.2).

Harrington (2002*) also used counts made between 1974 and 2000 by ISS cooperators to compare numbers of shorebirds at Delaware Bay to other Atlantic coastal regions (see section 5.2.3). From these counts, the maximum value of all counts of each species from Atlantic marine locations was determined for spring and fall migration periods. To compare Delaware Bay to other Atlantic locations, maximum counts made during 17 years of aerial surveys of Delaware Bay (see Clark et al. 1993) were divided by the sum of maximum counts made at sites surveyed by the International Shorebird Surveys (ISS). There were 483 Atlantic coast locations visited (13,987 surveys) during fall migration and 259 visited during spring (5,795 surveys); 19 of the locations visited during fall were on Delaware Bay. Maximum counts from these Delaware Bay sites were summed to provide an overall index for the bay. Because of duplication with aerial surveys, ISS counts made during spring at sites on Delaware Bay were excluded from evaluation. Delaware Bay provides important habitat to some migrant shorebirds during fall migration, but is particularly important in spring (Table 6.1). Aggregations in Delaware Bay were greater during spring than fall across all species, and were dramatically so for all species except dowitchers (Table 6.1). The difference between proportional use in spring and fall might be attributable to the fact that there were data from aerial surveys of Delaware Bay during the spring but not during the fall. However, locations covered by the ISS in the fall included all of the well-known shorebird sites on Delaware Bay. The differing methodology does not seem to explain the large seasonal differences. Even if the method did confound interpretation of results, it could not explain the seasonal shifts of relative occurrence between species. For example, turnstones, knots and sanderlings were virtually absent from Delaware Bay during fall, whereas semipalmated sandpipers, dowitchers and dunlin were conspicuously present during both seasons. Clearly, Delaware Bay is critical spring stopover for many shorebirds, and >50% of the flyway populations of ruddy turnstones, red knots, and semipalmated sandpipers may use Delaware Bay beaches. Reliable estimates of turnover rates could show an increased importance of Delaware Bay to these species. The comparisons described above are probably the most reliable, minimal estimate of use of Delaware Bay by migrant shorebird populations.

7.0. HABITAT USE BY SHOREBIRDS AND HORSESHOE CRABS

7.1. Shorebird Use of Marine and Non-marine Habitats

Harrington (2002*) used counts made between 1974 and 2000 by ISS cooperators to compare use of marine and non-marine sites along the Atlantic coast (see section 5.2.3). Survey sites were classified as primarily either marine or non-marine habitats and the average number of birds recorded during surveys was computed for northward and southward migration. Ruddy turnstones, red knots, sanderlings, dunlins, and short-billed dowitchers were all more abundant in marine than non-marine habitats during northward and southward migration (Table 7.1). Semipalmated sandpipers were more abundant in marine habitats in fall, but were equally abundant between marine and non-marine habitats during spring. Long-billed dowitchers and least sandpipers were equally abundant in both habitat types during both seasons (Table 7.1).

7.2. Red Knot Habitat Use and Movements in Delaware Bay

Meyer et al. (ND*) radio-tagged red knots taken from cannon-net catches on New Jersey beaches 15–19 May 1997 (5 birds) and on New Jersey (30 birds) and Delaware (20 birds) beaches 2–21 May 1998. Telemetric searches for radio-tagged birds were conducted from the ground 16–30 May in 1997 and from the ground and air 3 May–9 June 1998. Pre-determined ground locations were surveyed in New Jersey and Delaware; transmitter range averaged 1.6 km on the ground and 8 km in the air. Habitat, home range (kernels), and behavior was measured for each bird. Mean minimum duration of stay (calculated as the difference between initial capture day and day of last detection) in 1998 was 17 ± 8 days ($\pm$ SD, $\square$ = 47 birds) and ranged from 1 to 35 days. Birds may have been present in the bay for an unknown number of days before capture. Radio-tagged birds preferentially used the lower, rather than upper, Delaware Bay region (χ^2 = 317, df = 4, P = 0.001). The greatest number of radio-tagged birds were located in New Jersey on 16 May, whereas the greatest number of birds was detected in Delaware in 23 May. Radio-tagged birds were not distributed evenly among all beaches and marshes and were concentrated on a few beaches throughout the bay ($\chi^2 \geq 179$, df ≥ 22, P = 0.001) and also within each state. Radio-tagged red knots commonly crossed Delaware Bay; in 1998, 60% of radio-tagged knots made ≥ 1 bay crossing. The number of bay crossings an individual knot would make was independent of initial weight, banding date, minimum duration stay, capture location, number of re-sightings, or any interactions. Frequency of bay crossings increased at the end of the May. Knots moved on average 27.4 km (SD = 16.8). Significantly more knots were located on beaches than in marshes (χ^2 = 4,797, df = 1, P < 0.0001), and most knots were found on sandy beaches (79% of beach detections).

7.3. Shorebird Habitat Use on Cape May Peninsula, New Jersey

Burger et al. (1997) chose representative (non-random) marshes and beaches along the Atlantic and Delaware Bay coasts of New Jersey to determine shorebird numerical and behavioral use; the magnitude of shorebird use was a consideration in selection. Scan samples of shorebirds (20 minutes) were made from 22 May to 4 June, 1991–92, at 2 Atlantic Ocean marshes and 1 (each) marsh, mudflat, and beach along Delaware Bay. Surveys occurred during different tidal stages. Scans were considered independent (with no to few replicates in space) and multiple regression procedures (arc-sine transformations) were used to construct habitat models. Univariate tests (Kruskal-Wallis) were used to determine significance of individual variables. Burger et al. (1997) found that location, date, tide, time, species, and location-tide interaction were significant in explaining differences in the proportion of shorebirds that were alert, feeding, or resting. Shorebirds fed mainly on falling, low, and rising tides. More birds fed in marshes and on mudflats than on beaches, and a higher proportion of birds fed during the middle of migration than at the beginning or end. The mudflats had the highest number of birds and the greatest proportion of feeding shorebirds. Location was the most important factor that explained differences in feeding within species. Ruddy turnstones and red knots were found in greater than expected proportions in Atlantic marshes. The greatest number of semipalmated sandpipers, red knots, ruddy turnstones, and sanderlings foraged on a rising tide. They conclude that migrant shorebirds use a mosaic of habitats on the Cape May Peninsula, and that habitat switching likely occurs because of the need to feed.

7.4. Shorebird Beach Use in Delaware

Carter (2002*) used information opportunistically collected during field work to generate a preliminary map of beaches that supported the greatest numbers of red knots and ruddy turnstones in Delaware. Beach use was grouped into 4 categories: 1) extremely high use—large flocks at all weather conditions, 2) high use—large flocks in mild weather conditions, 3) moderate use—occasional large flocks intermittently, and 4) occasional use—some individuals, not regular. These criteria were applied to a 77-km length of shoreline between Woodland Beach and Cape Henlopen. Extremely high or high use beaches constituted 14% of the shoreline for red knots and 19% of the shoreline for ruddy turnstones (Table 7.2). Knots may distribute themselves among Delaware beaches in response (negatively) to on-shore wind speed. Carter and Scarborough (2002*) found that when average winds were >6.4 km/hour (over a 24-hour period measured at 5-second intervals), resultant wave heights deterred crab spawning and shorebird feeding on Delaware beaches. Information from radio-tagged knots is consistent with shorebird beach use data from Delaware and suggest that large aggregations of shorebirds are concentrated on a relatively small amount of Delaware Bay shoreline. Delineation and maintenance of high quality beach habitats for spawning crabs and foraging shorebirds is needed to ensure their long-term conservation.

7.5. Influence of Beach Characteristics on Horseshoe Crab Reproductive Activity

Smith et al. (2002b) surveyed 8 beaches each in New Jersey and Delaware to enumerate numbers of spawning crabs and deposited eggs. Beaches were selected in a stratified, random design based on (Smith et al. 2002c). For eggs, 5-cm cores were taken within a 3-m strip centered on the mid-beach elevation located along a 100-m segment of beach. At 40 locations on each beach, 2 core samples were taken (0–5 cm and 5–20 cm). Eggs sampled 24–25 May and 14–15

June, which corresponded to heaviest spawning in 1999, were used to calculate density. Spawning crab surveys follow a bay-wide procedure that uses a stratified randomization with beaches, times, and quadrats as sampling units. Temporal strata were 5-day periods around new and full moons in May and June. Beach lengths varied 200–1,000 m and were surveyed at night (the higher of the daily tides). Systematically placed quadrats, with random starts, of 1 m^2 were used to count spawning female crabs. A sub-sample from each beach that overlapped with egg sampling was used to compare spawning crab density and egg density. Egg clusters were sampled across the entire beach where crabs were observed spawning to determine spatial distribution of eggs. Beaches were ploughed by a tractor in Delaware to determine distribution of eggs clusters. Beach slope was incorporated into regression tree models, and Spearman rank correlations were also used.

Smith et al. (2002b) found that correlations between cumulative densities of spawning crabs and deposited eggs (total and surface) varied among time and beach. The interaction of wave action, beach morphology, and beach location has a large effect on the number of eggs that remain on a beach. Certain beaches could be critically important to shorebirds. Horseshoe crabs appear to prefer low-energy, sandy beaches. High, wide low-tide terraces dissipate wave energy and create narrow, steep beaches. Previously, Botton et al. (1988) had surveyed 80 km of New Jersey beaches in Delaware Bay and found that only a moderate percentage of the shoreline provided optimal (10.6%) or suitable (an additional 21.1%) spawning habitat for horseshoe crabs (31%, 26 km). Changing beach morphology could explain crabs spawning in tidal creeks. Association between beach morphology and live eggs on the surface was strong especially in late May. Distribution of eggs across beach foreshore was wider than previously reported. Egg distribution widened and became more uniform as the season progressed. They suggest that egg availability is not a simple function of number of females (but would be a minimum).

7.6. Beach Nourishment and Habitat Restoration for Crabs and Shorebirds

Because the value of beach nourishment may depend on beach geometry and type of sediment application, Smith et al. (2002a*) evaluated the response of spawning horseshoe crabs to nourishment treatments in Delaware. About 2.294 million m^3 of sand have been placed on Delaware Bay beaches in Delaware over the last 40 years. Re-nourishment efforts in New Jersey are less intense than in Delaware. Two beaches selected for nourishment were compared to 2 un-nourished beaches in a controlled before-after design in 2001–2002. Coarse-grained sediment, topped by a layer of pea gravel, were added to treatment beaches. Counts of spawning crabs and sediment cores were taken, following methods outlined by Smith et al. (2002b) above, at each treatment and control beach. Analysis of Variance was used to compare treatment and control groups. Topographic features of the beach were measured, and egg pouches were placed in beach sediments at 3 tidal elevations to determine moisture content. May crab spawning on nourished beaches increased between 2001 and 2002, whereas spawning decreased in control beaches. Spawning declined on all beaches in June but was most dramatic on control beaches. May total egg density on nourished beaches dramatically increased between 2001 and 2002, whereas increase on the control beach (egg counts were only made on 1 control beach) were less.

Egg density was substantially lower in 2002, relative to 2001, on all beaches. Beach characteristics, which influenced sediment moisture levels, affected egg development and viability. As preliminary conclusions, the authors suggest that nourishment can have a positive effect on horseshoe crab spawning if: 1) small volumes of nourished sediments are added that do not sufficiently alter beach slope, and 2) the application reflects a coarse estuarine beach that includes fine-grained sediments, gravel, and sand grains 0.35–0.50 mm in diameter. More information is needed to assess optimum size of fill materials and timing of operations.

7.7. Shorebird Habitat Use in Relation to Beach Characteristics and Abundance of Horseshoe Crabs and Their Eggs

Botton et al. (1994) selected (non-randomly) 7 beaches along the New Jersey coast of Delaware Bay to survey shorebirds, adult horseshoe crabs, and horseshoe crab eggs. Shoreline sites were selected to represent typical beach habitat types and varied in structure and amount of disturbance. Shorebirds were counted at sites, a variable number of times, at diurnal low, high, and mid-tide periods between mid-May and early June; small calidrids (virtually all semipalmated sandpipers) were combined as peeps to produce the metric of birds/observer/hour. Adult horseshoe crabs were counted in 3 ways: spawning crabs along transects parallel to the shoreline (high tide), nest bowl depressions created by spawning females (low tide), and stranded crabs (low tide). Sediments were sampled during 2 periods from late April to early May and from mid-May to early June, on 2 non-random transects perpendicular to the shoreline from mean low water to spring high tide, at 3-m interval stations on transects, and at 2 depths (0–5 cm and 15–20 cm). Numbers of all developmental stages of horseshoe crabs were counted and sand grain size was determined. Beach slope, beach width (mean low water to spring high tide), presence of sand dunes, proximity to salt marshes, and degree of human disturbance were also measured.

Red knots, ruddy turnstones, sanderlings, and small ⬜ ⬜▥▥▥sandpipers (virtually all semipalmated sandpipers) constituted ≥98% of Botton et al's. (1994) observations. Abundance of shorebirds, adult crabs, and egg densities varied among beaches. No direct, statistical comparisons were made between shorebird density and beach characteristics or horseshoe crab adult/egg abundance. The authors concluded that grain size was not a good predictor of site selection in shorebirds, and that horseshoe crab egg density alone did not predict shorebird abundance. Confounding factors include competition with gulls and that the food resource may be super-abundant (i.e. not limiting). Few other invertebrate foods were found in sediment samples, and a previous study (Botton 1984) found that bird predation did not deplete populations of a small bivalve. They suggest that shorebirds might be choosing beaches near salt marshes for supplemental feeding and roosting, or beaches where artificial or natural structures trap the longshore drift of horseshoe crab eggs.

8.0. ABUNDANCE AND TRENDS OF HORSESHOE CRAB EGGS

8.1. Bay-wide Egg Density in 1999

Pooler et al. (2003) collected sediment on 2 days in May and 2 days in June 1999 on 16 beaches—8 in New Jersey and 8 in Delaware. Sediment was collected by 5-cm diameter cores within a 3-m wide strip along a 100-m segment of beach; the strip was centered on the mid-beach. One core to 5 cm (shallow) and 1 core to 20 cm (deep) were collected at 40 randomly selected locations in each strip. Median densities were 3 (shallow) and 275 (deep) eggs/core; numbers per core are translated into densities (eggs/m^2) in Table 8.1. May density in shallow sediments was highly variable among beaches and ranged from 0 to 14,000 eggs/m^2. Total egg densities on Reed's Beach were lower in 1999 than 1990, but surrounding beaches in 1999 had similar egg densities as Reed's in 1990.

8.2. Egg Density on Delaware Beaches

During May 2001, Weber (2001*) sampled 8 beaches in Delaware on the new and full moons to determine horseshoe crab egg density. Two transects, placed perpendicular to the beach from foot of the beach up to 83% of the distance to the nocturnal high-tide wrack line were placed at each site (previous work has indicated all eggs were laid in this zone). Twenty-five cores (5.7-cm diameter by 20-cm length) were systematically sampled across these 2 transects at depths of 0–5 cm and 5–20 cm. Eggs were separated and either directly counted or estimated by volume. The extent of horseshoe crab spawning areas were delineated on each beach. Mean density of eggs for each transect was used to determine total egg load on each beach. Although Weber had sampled other beaches in previous years, information was not comparable because: 1) methods were altered in the period (from horizontal transects to vertical transects), 2) egg data were pooled across the entire April–July period, and 3) several beaches were nourished between sampling periods (studies were designed to determine effects of nourishment, see section 7.6). Densities in shallow sediments in May 2001 ranged from 873 to 530,000 eggs/m^2, and percentage of total eggs in shallow sediments ranged from 4 to 50% (Table 8.2). Only 3 of 8 beaches had densities that were >100,000 eggs/m^2 on either May sampling date. Repeated surveys of shallow egg abundance across the entire season at Port Mahon (a beach that did not undergo nourishment treatments) were similar among years [473,000 eggs (1999); 403,000 eggs (2000); 501,000 (2001); Weber 2002*].

8.3. Changes in Egg Density on New Jersey Beaches

Botton et al. (1994) reported that surface egg density, in the mid-beach, reached 10^4 to 10^5 eggs/m^2 in the early 1990s (see section 7.7 for details). Following their "pit" methods, Niles et al. (2003*) surveyed horseshoe crab eggs on 6 beaches in New Jersey (Moore's, Reed's, Cook's, Kimble's, Norbury's Landing, and Villas). Six samples, spaced 3-m apart were taken weekly (2 transects) across the tidal gradient on each beach. Nonparametric tests (Kruskal-Wallis) were used to determine differences among years. The number of horseshoe crab eggs in shallow sediments (0-5 cm) was not evenly distributed among years ($\chi^2 = 39.95$, df = 2, $P < 0.001$). By 2002, Niles et al. (2003*) reported densities of $\geq 10,000$ eggs/m^2 on fewer beaches ($\chi^2 = 15.32$, df = 2, $P < 0.0005$) and for a shorter time (χ^2, $P < 0.0001$). However, detailed information was not presented on changes in beach habitats during this period, egg densities on individual beaches, or parametric variance calculations provided in tables. Because egg density is known to be highly variable within and among beaches, additional details on methods and analytical calculations are needed before these data can be interpreted.

8.4. Egg Abundance Sampling Design Considerations

Pooler et al. (2003) addressed 3 specific questions needed to develop a statistical design to estimate the quantity of horseshoe crab eggs: 1) how many sediment samples are needed per beach segment, 2) is egg density in a segment representative of the entire beach, and 3) how many beaches are needed to estimate bay-wide density. Questions considered eggs in shallow (0–5 cm) and deep (0–20 cm) sediments (see section 8.2). Program TRENDS was used to determine power of detecting a decline at various coefficient of variation levels and a Type I error rate of 0.2. A sample size of 40 sediment cores was sufficient for estimating and monitoring density of eggs 0–20 cm deep within a 100-m beach segment. However, a larger sample size (60 sediment cores) would be needed for estimating and monitoring density of eggs 0–5 cm deep within a segment of beach. At most beaches, observed egg densities within the 100-m segment were not representative of egg densities throughout the larger beach. On only 2 of 6 New Jersey beaches did observed egg density fall within the inter-quartile range of beach-wide densities. Variability in egg densities among beaches tended to be higher in June for shallow (CV = 0.43) and deep (CV = 0.29) sediments than in May (CV = 0.33, 0.26). A two-stage (segment, cores) approach to sampling egg density is suggested. At least 10 segments per state would be needed to achieve a CV of 0.3 in shallow sediments.

9.0. SHOREBIRD DIET AND USE OF HORSESHOE CRAB EGGS

9.1. Shorebird Diet in Delaware Bay

Tsipoura and Burger (1999) collected gut samples from >100 shorebirds by stomach flushing during May 1996 and 1997. These samples were analyzed under a microscope to determine the type of prey that the birds ingested, and proportional composition was determined through volumetric measures. Horseshoe crab eggs were found in guts of all shorebird species captured on the mudflats and beaches of the Cape May Peninsula. For beaches on Delaware Bay, horseshoe crab eggs ranged about 95-100% for red knots ($\square$ = 21), 100% for ruddy turnstones ($\square$ = 6), 95–100% for sanderling ($\square$ = 13), 80–90% for semipalmated sandpipers ($\square$ = 30), and 60–100% for least sandpiper ($\square$ = 12) of invertebrate remains in the gut. Lower numbers of eggs were found in birds captured while foraging in the marsh (semipalmated sandpipers and least sandpipers) and along the Ocean shore (sanderlings). Worms, insects and detritus made up a higher percentage of gut contents in those habitats. Sand was ingested by all species in all habitats, indicating that it might be important in the digestion process. There were higher concentrations of horseshoe crab egg membranes in all gut samples collected in 1996 compared to 1997. Conversely, sanderling semipalmated sandpiper, and least sandpiper samples in 1997 had higher percentages of worms than in 1996.

9.2. Stable Isotope Analysis Confirms Shorebird Dependance on Horseshoe Crab Eggs in Delaware Bay

Haramis et al. (2002*) used stable isotope technology to establish the unique isotopic signature of horseshoe crab eggs and developed methods to determine the signature in shorebird tissue. Blood plasma was used because of rapid turnover that would yield a local diet-related stable isotope signature. Eggs and other invertebrate shorebird foods were sampled. Feeding trials of penned red knots and ruddy turnstones were also conducted to determine consumption rate, diet-tissue fractionation, and mass gains of birds fed only horseshoe crab eggs. The horseshoe crab egg signature was well-separated from other invertebrate foods (e.g., blue mussels, sand shrimp, amphipods) and would be traceable in shorebird tissue. Carbon and nitrogen plasma stable isotope signatures of red knots (n = 48) were centered around the horseshoe crab egg value. Variability in isotope values was likely due to some consumption of non-egg invertebrate foods. Regression of the plasma nitrogen with body mass converged on the crab egg value. Body mass was a strong correlate of feeding time on crab eggs (n = 42). Knots held in a pen (n = 10) initially lost weight (first 9 days in captivity) and then entered a 13-day period of rapid weight gain; birds gained an average of 33.5 g (29.4%) of body weight during this period. Birds fed horseshoe crab eggs ad libitum during daylight conditions consumed an average of 18,000 eggs/day. On Delaware Bay beaches, this translates to about 1 egg/second for a 5-hour period. One bird, the lightest at capture, gained 50% of its body weight over 13 days. Mass gains of captive birds exceeded 6 g/day, a rate comparable to that measured in live-trapped birds in Delaware Bay. These findings clearly demonstrate the red knot dependence on horseshoe crab eggs by convergence of isotope signature to the egg value, weight gains correlated with time feeding on crab eggs, and weight gains of caged birds solely fed crab eggs matched rate of weight gain in free-living knots. Data is currently being analyzed for other species (ruddy turnstones, semipalmated sandpipers, and least sandpipers).

9.3. Functional Responses of Shorebirds Feeding on Horseshoe Crab Eggs

Stillman et al. (2003*) measured the feeding rates of shorebirds in response to horseshoe crab egg density. Eggs were mixed with sand in a shallow tray ($\approx$0.3 m^2, 2-cm deep) and presented to shorebirds on Delaware beaches. Egg density in treatments varied from 300/m^2 to 25,000/m^2. Foraging behavior of focal shorebirds was video-recorded for 5 minutes after the first bird entered the tray area. All interactions between birds were recorded. The numbers of shorebirds in the tray were counted at 15-second intervals. After 5 minutes, the tray was retrieved and the sand-egg mixture removed for later separation. Attack rate, assessed by each time a bird pecked the sand surface, was calculated, during the first 1 minute of the tape, for dunlins, semipalmated sandpipers, and red knots. Densities of birds feeding within and outside of trays were thought to be similar, and the average density of feeding shorebirds during the 5-minute interval was positively, linearly correlated to egg substrate density ($P < 0.001$). After 5 minutes, birds tended to deplete about 80% of the eggs, regardless of either species or egg density. Pecking rates were similar among species (1.7/second for semipalmated sandpipers; 2.0/second for red knots and dunlins) and did not vary with egg density (linear regression; $\square =$ 30, 28, 11; $P > 0.05$). Because direct consumption could not be measured, the probability of consuming an egg given a peck was calculated by determining the total number of pecks in each experiment (the number of bird seconds*species-specific pecking rate) and the number of eggs per peck (total number of eggs consumed/total number of pecks). The number of eggs per peck increased from near 0 to 1 when density was >10,000 eggs/m^2 and was described as p = (p_{max}*E)/(E_{50}+E), where p = number of eggs consumed per peck, E = initial egg density, E_{50} = egg density at which p is 50% of p_{max}. Values were estimated as 3,355 (E_{50}) and 1.3 (p_{max}) from non-linear regression ($P < 0.05$). The number of eggs consumed per peck was not influenced by species composition on the feeding tray. Feeding rate (F) of each species was calculated as: F = aE/(1+aEH), where a = area search rate (m^2/second) and H = handling time. Estimates of a and H from non-linear regression were: 0.00069 m^2/second and 0.45 second for semipalmated sandpipers; 0.00083 m^2/second and 0.38 second for dunlins; and 0.00094 m^2/second and 0.38 second for knots. Interference was not included in the model, and data supported the rarity of aggressive interactions among feeding shorebirds. Feeding rate for all 3 shorebirds showed a similar positive, logarithmic relationship with egg density. At the highest egg densities (25,000 eggs/m^2), shorebirds fed at a rate of 2 eggs/second. Despite vast body size differences of the 3 shorebird species, feeding rates were similar. Maintenance of a feeding rate of 1 egg/second for 5 hours would lead to a daily consumption similar to estimates from feeding trials of penned knots (18,000 eggs, see section 9.2). Because energy expenditures are related to body mass, then mass gain beyond maintenance in larger-bodied birds (e.g., red knot) might only be possible if horseshoe crab eggs are available in high densities. Knots should be the first species to exhibit reduced mass gains if horseshoe crab egg abundances are reduced.

9.4. Competition Between Shorebirds and Gulls for Horseshoe Crab Eggs

Gulls foraging on the beaches of Delaware Bay may directly or indirectly compete with shorebirds for horseshoe crab eggs. Burger et al. (1979) found that intraspecific aggressive interactions of shorebirds were more common than interspecific interactions. Negative interactions between knots and laughing gulls that resulted in disruption of knot behavior were no more prevalent than interactions with ruddy turnstones, dowitchers, or black-bellied plovers (P□□□□□□□□□□□□□□□). However, larger bodied species tended to successfully defend areas against smaller species. Total aggressive interactions increased as density of birds increased in favored habitats, which indicated some competition for food resources. Sullivan (1986) found that aggression in ruddy turnstones increased as experimentally-manipulated food resources (horseshoe crab eggs) changed from an even distribution to a more patchy distribution. Decisions to defend food patches were likely driven by the cost of locating new patches.

Following upon earlier results, Burger et al. (2003*) studied foraging behavior in shorebirds and gulls at Delaware Bay, New Jersey, during spring migration to determine if interference competition existed between shorebirds and gulls. They tested the hypothesis that vigilance and aggression rates (and thus foraging rates) were directly related to the size of the species of the nearest neighbor to foraging shorebirds. Thus, they make the prediction that vigilance and aggression rates will be greater when a shorebird's nearest neighbor is a gull, and that foraging rates are lower when the nearest neighbor to a shorebird is a gull. Interference competition occurs in foraging flocks if there is a change in feeding rate of a focal bird when it feeds in the presence of different numbers of competitors, or with different species. In general, shorebirds have conspecifics as their nearest neighbors and, thus, fed in conspecific groups. Similarly, laughing gulls usually fed among conspecifics.

The species of nearest neighbor has a significant effect on time spent foraging and number of pecks (per 30 seconds) of ruddy turnstones and laughing gulls (Table 9.2). For knots and turnstones, however, the time devoted to foraging when gulls were present was significantly less than when a nearest neighbor was any shorebird (Table 9.2). In addition, the mean number of pecks/30 seconds was significantly less when turnstones and sanderlings had gulls as nearest neighbors (Table 9.2). Besides actually feeding, foraging shorebirds engage in aggressive and vigilant behaviors. Red knots, turnstones, and to some extent dowitchers, spent more time being vigilant when their nearest neighbors were gulls rather than other shorebirds (Table 9.2). Similarly, knots, turnstones and semipalmated sandpipers engaged in more aggression when gulls were nearest neighbors (although they usually lost).

Reduction of available horseshoe crab eggs or consolidation of spawning crabs onto fewer beaches could increase interference competition among egg foragers. Botton et al. (1994) noted that flocks of shorebirds appeared to be deterred from landing on beaches when large flocks of gulls were present. Maximum counts of gulls foraging along the New Jersey shoreline of Delaware Bay, however, may not have increased over the last decade, whereas breeding counts of laughing gulls (□□□□□□□□□□□□) in Atlantic coast marshes may have increased (Table 9.1; L. Niles unpublished data). Details on survey methods are not provided.

9.5. Red Knots Use of Food Other than Horseshoe Crab Eggs

Away from Delaware Bay, red knots primarily feed on molluscs and bivalves. Harrington and Winn (2001*) noted that prey of Georgia coast red knots were likely dwarf surf clams (□ □□□□□□ □□□□□□□), and knots in South Carolina fed mainly on coquina clams (□ □□□□□□□□□□□). Food resources available to knots on the Virginia coast, where knot densities were highest, were blue mussels (□ □□□□□□□□□□) and Melitid amphipods (Truitt et al. 2001*). Preliminary information presented by Escudero and Niles (2001*) suggests that invertebrates in many Atlantic coast habitats are not dense enough to support the energetic needs of red knots. In samples of 7 New Jersey beaches, Botton et al. (1994) found that density of surface macroinvertebrates was seldom >200/m^2 and there were no significant differences in invertebrate density among beaches. Night feeding, use of alternative foods, and foraging patch residence time have been suggested as the behavioral modifications that demonstrate the inability of knots to meet their energetic requirements solely through horseshoe crab egg consumption (Sitters 2001*). Preliminary evidence suggests these behaviors are being used by knots, but lack of a historical perspective questions their significance. More detailed studies of prey quality (i.e. energy density) and quantity in the Delaware Bay region are needed to assess the significance of alternative prey, including assessment of temporal and spatial variation in prey abundance.

González et al. (1996) studied the foraging ecology of red knots feeding on restingas at San Antonio Oeste, Argentina. Behavior of birds was recorded and fecal samples were collected, weighed, and analyzed to determine sizes and biomass of mussels (*Brachidontes rodriguezi*) ingested by knots. Mussel density and biomass were measured for 3 areas where feces were collected. Ash and ash-free dry mass were determined from samples to predict biomass of equivalent of droppings. Ivlev's electivity index was used to determine if knots were selecting certain size classes. Defecation rates (droppings/bird-minute) were determined for a small area of a restinga. Numbers of knots fluctuated between 0 and 12,000 individuals in the area, and flocks tended to spend about 6–8 days at the stopover. Knots made repeated jabs to capture appropriately sized mussels and handling times were short (1–2 seconds). Mussel density ranged from 1,800 to 6,000 individuals (per m^2) which included 60–80% of sizes appropriate for ingestion by knots (5–20 mm, mean = 10.3 mm). Mussel biomass followed patterns of mussel density. Knot droppings exclusively contained mussels. Mean defecation rate of knots was 0.42 droppings/bird-minute. This translated into an intake rate of 0.433 mg ash-free dry mass/second. *Brachidontes* mussels are rather slender and therefore ingestable by knots. Breaking forces of larger *Brachidontes* were less than similar-sized *Mytilus*. Optimistic projections suggest that knots may gain 5 g/day feeding on mussels. This refueling rate would allow fat accumulation to reach the next stopover in Brazil. Sitters et al. (2001) studied nocturnal distributions and foraging in radio-tagged red knots at a migratory stopover site near San Antonio Oeste, Argentina, during northward migration in and March and April 1998, and found that knots fed in habitats at night that differed from diurnal feeding sites. Previously González et al. (1996) reported that red knots cannot meet their daily requirements solely by feeding during the day. Brayton and Schneider (2000) found that the magnitude of shorebird use of beaches on the Peninsula Valdez, Argentina, did not correspond with prey density. Tidal exposure time was the best predictor of shorebird use. Gizzard and fecal analysis of red knots conducted at Punta Rasa, Argentina, in 1995 and 2000 (Alemany et al. 2001*) indicated that mudsnails (*Heleobia australis*), in the range of 1–3.5 mm in length, were the main prey taken.

10.0 ENERGETIC REQUIREMENTS OF MIGRANT SHOREBIRDS

10.1. An Energetics Framework for Migrant Shorebirds

An energy based conceptual framework presented by Piersma (1996), was an effort to integrate research on energy intake and energy expenditure of birds. A shorebird's energy budget consists of energy intake on the one side and energy expenditures on the other. Higher energy expenditures require higher energy intake. The energy expenditures consist of: 1) the Basal Metabolic Rate (BMR)—the energy consumed by a bird at rest, 2) the cost of thermoregulation—the energy required to maintain body temperature in lower temperatures, which will be higher with decreasing ambient temperature, 3) the cost of activity, and 4) the heat increment of feeding—the energy used in the digestive and assimilation process. The energy intake depends on the food and rate at which food can be consumed. For a specific diet item, functional response curves can describe the relationship between food abundance and food intake rates. For a diet consisting mainly of one food item (e.g., red knots foraging solely on *Maco□a balthica* in the Dutch Wadden Sea), it is relatively easy to estimate the required intake rates and prey biomass needed to counterbalance the energy demands. However, these relationships become more complicated when a variety of prey items are consumed. The balance of the intake versus output is not constant throughout the year but differs depending on the season. For example, the balance is positive (energy stored) during preparation for migration, whereas the balance is strongly negative for a few days during long-distance flights (energy consumed with no intake).

10.2. Energetics of Sanderlings Migrating to Four Latitudes

Castro et al. (1992) studied sanderlings that spend the winter at 4 different latitudes to quantify the energetic costs incurred by wintering at different latitudes. The study included measurements of daily energy expenditure, fat levels, and time budgets of sanderlings in New Jersey, Texas, Panama, and Peru. Daily energy expenditure was measured by injecting doubly labeled water into captured birds, releasing them in the wild, and finally calculating energy used from blood samples from these birds 24 hours later. No information is provided on the effects of handling. The collected birds were then analyzed to determine body composition and fat levels. Finally, time budgets were calculated by observing the activities of flocks of birds at all 4 locations, but behavior of the group may not necessarily be representative of the sampled individuals. Thermal environment explained 70% of the variance in sanderlings daily energy expenditure, with energy cost being twice as high in New Jersey as in Panama, and somewhere in between in Texas and Peru. Similarly, body mass and fat reserves of sanderlings were inversely correlated with air temperatures across sites. Sanderlings at all locations spent most of their time feeding or roosting. Time budgets between sites, with the exception of Texas, were similar and suggests that shorebirds manage to fulfill their living costs despite the high daily energy cost of the cold New Jersey winter.

10.3. Predicting Flight Ranges

Castro and Myers (1988) developed equations to determine the cost of flight of shorebirds that were based on body mass and morphometric variables related to flight. These equations were statistically derived by regression of measured energy costs of flight, for a variety of species of birds, against body mass, wing length, wing span, and wing area. The model with the best fit included only 2 parameters—body mass and wing length. Compared to the models developed by Raveling and Lefebvre (1967) and Kendeigh (1977), the equations of Castro and Myers (1988) predict increasing costs of flight with increasing body mass. This discrepancy occurred because the other 2 models used allometric equations to predict cost flight as a simple function of body mass without taking aerodynamic design into consideration. Based on these equations, and allowing for loss in body mass during flight, Castro and Myers (1989) estimated the flight ranges of 6 species of shorebirds. The model can be expressed in the following equation: $R = 26.88*S*L^{1.614}*(M_1^{-0.464} - M_2^{-0.464})$, where R = flight range (km), M_1 = body mass at end of flight (g), M_2 = body mass at the start (g), S = flight speed (km/h) and L = wing length (cm). Flight range estimates were determined based on the assumption of a 75 km/hour flight speed. Castro and Myers (1989) predict that although larger shorebirds can store more fat reserves, the flight distance is similar for large and small shorebird species. Using the Castro and Myers (1989) model, red knots would have depart Delaware Bay at a weight of 197 g to fly 2,400 km to arctic Canada and have 5 days worth of energy stores upon arrival. Mizrahi (1999) found that some Delaware Bay semipalmated sandpipers did not have enough fat reserves to reach breeding areas in James Bay and Labrador, Canada, and others were predicted to arrive with few (<1.0 g) reserves. Semipalmated sandpipers were very selective about wind conditions during departure, a behavior used to maximize flight energy efficiency.

10.4. Fat-loading in *islandica* Red Knots

According to flight mechanics theory, flight costs increase with increasing body mass, and migrants should therefore avoid carrying large fat reserves. However, if migrants are under time constraints, such as the need to reach the breeding grounds as early as possible, they may need to carry heavier fat loads than those predicted based on energetic costs. Gudmundsson et al. (1991) present a theoretical framework to predict whether the birds are adapted to minimize energy or time spent on migration. During spring migration, when the birds are moving north, they are moving from staging sites with better and more predictable resources, which allow for fast fat deposition, to areas that are lesser quality feeding habitats. Under this scenario it is preferable to overload on fat reserves at sites that are richer in prey and by-pass the poorer ones. The authors present specific information for knots, turnstones and sanderlings captured in Iceland during northbound migration. At this site: knots depart at an mean body mass of 205.1 ± 1.9 (SE) g (*n* = 30; corresponding to 53.1% fat load), sanderlings depart at 82.6 ± 1.2 (SE) g (*n* = 36; a 53% fat load), and ruddy turnstones depart at 161.6 ± 2.4 (SE) g (*n* = 47 a 53.9% fat load). Based on these fat energy stores, flight ranges were estimated, and most shorebirds had greater fat loads than those required to complete their migration. These overloads may represent a time minimization strategy or a risk insurance against unfavorable conditions in other staging areas or the breeding grounds. Kvist et al. (2001), however, found that flight is not as metabolic expensive as originally thought (see next section).

10.5. Effects of Weight on Metabolic Power Needed for Flight

Kvist et al. (2001) experimentally investigated whether the predicted mechanical output required by increasing weight is reflected in increases in the metabolic energy input of birds in flight. They measured metabolic power input of 4 red knots during 28 flights in a wind tunnel using doubly labeled water. Metabolic power input during flight was calculated from CO_2 production after correcting for energy that would be spent if the bird was not flying (1.5*basal metabolic rate). The metabolic power input increased allometrically with increasing body weight, with an exponent of 0.35. The flight muscle efficiency estimated from the measured power input and the predicted mechanical output also increased with increasing fuel load. This research indicates that red knots may maintain flight muscles at optimal size to decrease the energy requirements of migration. Therefore, the cost of carrying an additional unit of fuel may be lower than assumed in current models of bird migration. Muscle efficiency changes for migration may be incompatible with muscles structure changes needed for short transient flights, such as those needed to avoid predation. These results indicate a dynamic body mass model is needed to predict flight energy needs.

10.6. Flight Energy Needs of *rufa* Red Knots Staging in Delaware Bay

Baker et al. (2003) determined if energetic stress during refueling was negatively affecting adult red knots in Delaware Bay. They assumed a 180 g average mass over the duration of a minimal flight of 2,400 km to Southampton Island and that energy can be predicted as $\log_{10}$ power (W) = $0.39 + 0.35 \log_{10}$ body mass (g), which is based on wind tunnel experiments of Kvist et al. (2001). Solving this equation yields a flight cost of 15W which translates into 54 kJ/hour. If the energy density of fat is 40 kJ/g, migrating birds will consume 1.35 g fat/hour. At a flight speed of 70 km/hour (Piersma et al. 1997), a flight of 2,400 km would require 47 g of fat. Maintenance on arrival would require 6.5 g/day (Piersma 2000). Based on lean mass of 130 g, departure weights of 180 g are minimal to cover migration to the arctic.

10.7. Assimilation Efficiency of Sanderlings Consuming Horseshoe Crab Eggs

Castro et al (1989) experimented with captive sanderlings to determine the assimilation efficiency of captive birds fed a horseshoe crab egg diet. Eight sanderlings were captured in Delaware Bay in early May. These birds were kept in individual cages with a wire mesh floor and fed ad libitum an exclusive diet of horseshoe crab eggs. Horseshoe crab eggs for the feeding experiments were collected in the field, washed to remove debris and sand, and kept frozen. Mealworms were obtained commercially. Three experimental feeding trials were conducted during which the birds were fed horseshoe crab eggs, and 1 feeding trial during which the birds were fed mealworms. During those experiments the food consumed and excreta were collected and weighed. Collected samples were dried and analyzed to determine lipid, nitrogen, carbon, and energy content. On average, each sanderling ingested 30.9 g of eggs or 8,300 eggs/day. The eggs passed through the gastrointestinal tract in 63 minutes. The birds did not gain any weight during the 4 weeks of the experiment and their metabolic efficiencies were exceedingly low (39%). When the birds were switched to a diet of mealworms, the assimilation efficiency improved significantly (75%) and became more typical of the assimilation efficiency of birds eating foods of animal origin. While on the mealworm diet, the birds gained weight. However, large numbers of horseshoe crab eggs passed through the sanderlings' digestive tract undigested. Metabolic efficiency corrected for unbroken eggs that are not assimilated was actually 69%, much closer to what would normally be expected. The sanderlings also consumed significantly higher amounts of food, as measured by dry mass influx, on the crab egg diet compared to the mealworm diet. Based on these results the authors suggest that the birds are taking advantage of the sheer abundance of eggs to maximize the rate of metabolizable energy intake. One of the issues raised in this research was the fact that a high proportion of eggs (71.9%) passed thought the digestive tract of sanderlings undigested. However, the eggs that the birds were fed had been washed, eliminating the presence of sand that grinds the egg membranes and enables fuller digestion of hard items. In actual field conditions, one might expect that the assimilation efficiency will be higher than 39% and might approach the 69% estimate of metabolic efficiency corrected for unbroken eggs. Both Tsipoura and Burger (1999) and Piersma (2000) found sand and gravel in the guts of red knots, which suggests assimilation efficiency could be as high as 70%.

10.8. Energy budget of Delaware Bay Shorebirds

Castro and Myers (1993) calculated the total energy consumption of shorebirds during spring stopover in Delaware Bay by estimating total energy requirements and correcting for assimilation efficiency of ingested food. To determine energy expenditure, basal metabolic rates (BMRs) were calculated based on the equations for shorebirds of Kersten and Piersma (1987). Daily energy expenditure was assumed to be 2.5*BMR based on doubly labeled water measurements on sanderlings (Castro and Myers 1988). Total energy expenditure was obtained by multiplying the daily energy expenditure by 21, assuming that the mean number of days shorebirds stay in Delaware Bay is about 3 weeks. Energy stored as fat was calculated assuming that shorebirds depart Delaware Bay at body fat levels of 40%. The populations of 6 species of shorebirds (ruddy turnstones, red knots, sanderlings, semipalmated sandpipers, dunlin, and dowitchers) using Delaware Bay during spring migration were included in this calculation. The authors estimated that total energy requirement for all species using Delaware Bay is 2,133 x 10^6 kJ. Total energy consumption for all species, assuming an assimilation efficiency of 38.6% [(the assimilation efficiency measured by Castro et al. (1989) for sanderlings feeding on horseshoe crabs; see below], is 5,526 x 10^6 kJ. This is equivalent to 539 metric tons of horseshoe crab eggs.

10.9. Horseshoe Crab Egg Requirement of Delaware Bay Shorebirds

If calculations by Castro and Myers (1993) are updated with information gathered since their publication [fat gains adjusted from the uniform 40% to 45% for red knots, 50% for ruddy turnstones, and 70% for sanderling (see sections in 9.0); assimilation efficiency is increased to 70% (see section 10.7); and mean length of stay is reduced to 17 days (see section 7.2)], then total energy consumption by the 6 main species of shorebirds that use Delaware Bay beaches (ruddy turnstones, red knots, sanderlings, semipalmated sandpipers, dunlin, and dowitchers) would be 303 metric tons of horseshoe crab eggs (see Table 10.1). This does not account for any consumption by other shorebird species or other egg predators. Using Castro et al.'s (1989) energetic analysis, Botton et. al. (1994) suggested that egg densities were sufficient to support the entire Delaware Bay shorebird population (44,000 eggs/m^2), and that beaches had the ability to support the numbers of shorebirds observed there. However, they assumed that all 160 km of Delaware Bay's shoreline would provide foraging habitat for shorebirds and egg densities applied to a 20.8 m width of beach. Information on distribution of shorebirds and horseshoe crabs indicates that beaches of the upper bay are generally not used. If a minimum of 303 metric tons of eggs were required and suitable shoreline was reduced by a third to 120 km, a mid-beach surface density of 32,688 eggs/m^2 (20.8-m beach width) to 67,991 eggs/m^2 (10-m beach width) would be needed to support the spring flight of shorebirds (423,000 birds). If the average daily consumption rate of eggs is 18,000 per day, the egg requirement is: 423,000 total shorebirds in Delaware Bay*14-day stay in the bay (the period of maximum egg consumption)*18,000 eggs consumed per day = 1.07 x10^{11} eggs (42,707 eggs/m^2, 20.8-m width). If red knots consumed 18,000 eggs/day (see section 9.2), for 17 days, they would meet the energetic requirements of daily maintenance and adding an average of 5.23 g/day of fat during their stay in Delaware Bay (see Piersma 2000). Total red knot egg requirement would be 1.54*10^{10} eggs, which is within the same magnitude as the estimate Castro and Myers (1993) generated (1.75*10^{10} eggs), and suggests that the egg requirement derived above (1.07 x10^{11} eggs) could be realistic.

Clearly, reliable data on egg availability is one of the most important information needs in Delaware Bay with regards to the status of shorebirds. No beaches surveyed 25–26 May 1999 in either New Jersey or Delaware had shallow sediment (0–5 cm) densities that were >33,000 eggs/m^2 and only 4 of 16 beaches had densities >10,000 eggs/m^2 (see Table 8.1). Total sediment (0–20 cm) densities, however, were >33,000 eggs/m^2 on 11 of 16 beaches surveyed. On 25 May 2001, 2 of 7 beaches in Delaware had shallow sediment densities of >33,000 eggs/m^2 and 5 of 7 beaches ha densities of >10,000 eggs/m^2 (see Table 8.2). Sediment cores were collected during peaks of crab spawning in both years. More information on the temporal and spatial distribution of surface eggs is needed to determine if enough eggs are available to meet the energetic needs of foraging shorebirds. The wide variability in existing data on surface egg availability and the uncertainties surrounding beach dynamics and egg movement precludes drawing firm conclusions about whether or not shorebirds can satisfy their seasonal energetic requirements from horseshoe crab eggs.

11.0. SHOREBIRD WEIGHTS AND WEIGHT GAIN

11.1. General Capture Methods

For studies of weight gain and survival, shorebirds are captured by either mist, cannon, or woosh nets during May and, occasionally, early June. Captured birds are placed in opaque holding cages (to reduce stress) where they await processing. Red knots lost about 3 g/hour during repeated measurements of held birds (Gillings 2002*). All birds are banded (ringed) with a metal band, and some receive a complement of color bands and flags. Birds are weighed, either by electronic balance or Pesola spring scale (mainly 1997), and some are measured for wing length, culmen length, fat score, and other characters. Plumage (% breeding), molt, and age are sometimes recorded. All birds are usually processed within 4 hour of capture. No random selection of capture sites is used or is there any systematic attempt to distribute catches sites along a north-south beach gradient. No information exists on how individual capture probability changes within season or across seasons. Catches vary in their composition relative to behavior, roosting or feeding, of captured birds. In Delaware Bay, 95 catches were made between 1997 and 2002, and 52 catches yielded ≥50 red knots. From these catches, 9,692 red knots, 7,755 sanderlings, and 10,106 ruddy turnstones were weighed. Samples varied in both time and space, which could lead to interpretation problems with the data. Most of the catches (73%) from 1997 to 2002 were made on 2 beaches in Delaware (Mispillion Harbor and Slaughter Beach) and 2 beaches in New Jersey (Cook's and Reed's Beaches; Table 11.1). Among years, the contribution of these sites to the overall capture varied between 36 and 100%, and the total number captured ranged from 893 to 2,431 knots (Table 11.1–2). Temporal distribution of catches also varies among years (Table 11.2), and netting did not begin until 22 May in 1997.

11.2. Organ Atrophy and Weight Change during Migration

Changes in body mass and physiology during migration are not simply the result of changes in fat reserves. Muscle tissue and organs also undergo considerable fluctuations in mass (Lindström and Piersma 1993). To elucidate the changes in organ size during migratory stopover, Piersma (2000) randomly collected 6 Delaware Bay red knots on 4 dates in May 1998. Baker et al. (2003) compared birds captured on 28 May 1998 (6 females) to knots captured on 29 May 1999 (2 males, 6 females) and on 25 May 2000 (1 male, 6 females). Previous work demonstrated no body size differences between males and females (Piersma et al. 1999). Carcasses were frozen and at a later date, body composition and morphological measures were made. Tissues were excised, dried, weighed, and fat-free mass was determined. Between 6 and 14 May 1998, knots gained weight at 1.165 g/day, when virtually no fat was added. During the next 9 days, weight was gained at a rate of 6.391 g/day, and fat was added at 4.157 g/day. In the last 5 days, weight increased at 5.577 g/day and fat accumulated at 4.47 g/day. Most muscles slowly increased weight over the first 8 days and increased rapidly over the next 9 days. During the period of rapid weight gain, pectoral muscles increased by 50%, the heart increased by 40%, and leg muscles increased by 45%. The heart decreased slightly during the last 5 days before departure. Organs (Stomach, intestine, kidneys, liver) also increased dramatically (>50%) and stabilized during the last 5 days before departure. The lungs and spleen did not change mass during the period, but the salt glands mass increased steadily. Stomach contents indicated consumption of small stones, which would aid digestion of horseshoe crab eggs. Gradual changes in organs suggests that there was not a large pulse of recent arrivals in late May. These results were similar to studies of *islandica* knots at an Iceland spring staging site except that exercise organs increased in weight during the mid-period of migration (rather than at the end as in Iceland) and heart size declined prior to departure (Piersma et al. 1999). The vast changes in muscles and organs illustrate the importance of a high quality stopover, beyond fat deposition, for meeting energetic demands of migrating red knots. Information on other species in Delaware Bay is not currently available. Comparisons among years showed no significant differences in body size, body mass, total fat mass, or most organs and muscles (Baker et al. 2003). The only significant differences ($\square < 0.02$) were that fat-free mass of pectoral muscles and the intestine was lower in 1999 (compared to 1998 and 2000) and that liver size was reduced in 1999 and 2000 (compared to 1998). Reductions in these muscles and organs could compromise short- and long-term health of knots. In Delaware Bay, lean semipalmated sandpipers exhibited modulation of circulating corticosterone levels when exposed to stress (Mizrahi et al. 2000). Chronic levels of corticosterone can have a catabolic effect on striated muscle tissue, and this modulation may protect flight muscle structure during long-distance flights.

11.3. Red Knot Weights through the Annual Cycle

As is characteristic of most migratory shorebirds, weights of red knots vary substantially throughout life history stages (Harrington 2001). Mass of red knots wintering in Tierra del Fuego ranges from about 120 to 135 g (Baker et al. 1998). Knots visiting one of the first known stopover sites during northward migration, Peninsula Valdez, Argentina, did not increase mass between 11 and 20 April. In Rio Negro Province, Argentina, Gonzáles et al. (1996) showed that knots during March were consuming mussels (*Brachidontes* spp.) at a rate that would enable a mean mass increase of <1 g/day. During early April, knots with partial or complete alternate plumage at Punta Rasa, in Buenos Aires Province, Argentina, had a mean mass of 139 g (138.9 ± 16.9, n = 30) that was significantly heavier than basic-plumaged individuals (mean = 110.0 ± 7.9 g, n = 7). Body mass of adult and juvenile knots (n = 678) caught in Argentina during February and March 1997 was 120 g, and few birds weighed >140 g (Baker et al. 1998). During early May 1984, mean mass in southern Brazil was 202.2 g, the heaviest ever recorded for a sample of *ru⬚a* red knots. Basic-plumaged birds weighed significantly less than alternate-plumaged birds (155.0 g; Harrington et al. 1986). Nascimento (2001*) found that average weight of knots in May at Lagoa do Peixe was 192 g (n = 309, SD = 27). Knots generally gained weight from early to late April at Lagoa do Peixe (Baker et al. 1998). Further north on the Maranhão coast, the mean weight of knots captured in May was 153.6 g (range = 115–210 g, SD = 29.7), which suggests individuals may need to either gain weight or remain there for the boreal summer (Nascimento 2001). In the São Luís, Brazil, area, flocks were a mix of basic-plumaged, light-weight (assumed) sub-adults (mean = 140.1 g, SD = 10.1, n = 18) and heavier, alternative-plumaged adults (observed birds; Wilson et al. 1998). At Delaware Bay in the U. S., there was little change in mass before the third week of May (e.g., mean = 153.1 ± 20.8, n = 129 on 19 May), but a rapid increase during the last 10 days of the month (e.g., mean = 175.9 ± 17.5 g, n = 265 on 24 May; Harrington 2002). Knot weight needed for a successful flight to the arctic is thought to be at least 180 g (Piersma 2000). Threshold weights are suggested as 150 g for ruddy turnstones and 80 g for sanderlings (Gudmonsson et al. 1991). The mean weight of red knots measured 10 days after arrival on Southampton Island breeding grounds was 131.9 g (n = 18 knots captured at nests). Four of the 18 knots weighed were below the lean mass value (120 g; Niles et al. 2001*).

11.4. Red Knot Weight Gains in Delaware Bay

11.4.1. Analytical approaches

Robinson et al. (2003*) used complementary analyses of mean weights of captured birds and of birds which were captured more than once during a season to determine patterns of weight gain. Although weight was correlated to body size, no systematic patterns of differential sizes in catches on different dates were evident. Wing lengths were not available for all samples, and weights were therefore generally not corrected for body size. Individual red knot cohorts (which were groups of birds characterized by different arrival dates) were identified with techniques for decomposing multiple Gaussian curves (with the FAO-ICLARM Fish Stock Assessment Tools package). The general notion is that weights are normally distributed after the arrival of a single flock and become multi-modal as other groups of birds arrive. This approach accounts for yearly differences in timing of arrival and departure. If samples are large, analysis of same-year individually re-captured birds is the ideal way to determine weight changes. Because capture effects can depress weight change over a short period of time, a minimum recapture period of 7 days was used.

Niles et al. (2003*) estimated arrival and departure mass by taking the mean mass of the lowest- and highest-mass catches at the beginning and end of the season. The earliest catch was always used to determine arrival mass (generally >30 birds), but the mean departure mass may not have always been the latest catch. Multiple regression models were used to examine the influence of year, day, body size (bill, head, and flattened wing length), holding time, and time of capture on bird mass. Weight data were log_{10}-transformed to meet assumptions of variance homogeneity. Because catch effort at the beginning and end of the season varied the most among years, analyses were restricted to 14–28 May. Daily rate of mass gain was derived from the regression coefficient of "day" in the regression model. Mass change was not computed for individual birds, but was considered a crude rate of mass gain of all birds across the season. Body size variables were only used in models of mass gain in knots, and time of capture was insignificant in models of sanderling mass gain. Regression results were compared to mean mass of catches at 3-day intervals for full and reduced (day only) for each year. Comparisons were also made to predicted rates of mass change from the full model. The proportion of the maximum number of shorebirds present on weekly aerial surveys was included as a covariate in regression analyses of crude rate of mass gain. Separate comparisons were made for New Jersey and Delaware sides of the bay.

11.4.2. Red knot arrival weights and weight gains

Mean arrival weight (± SE) was 114.9 ± 1.6 g and was 12% below lean weight (Robinson et al. 2003*). Mean arrival weight, across comparable years, ranged from 105.0 ± 8.8 g (2000) to 120.0 ± 11.1 g (2001); the lowest arrival weight recorded was 85.9 g (30% below lean mass; Niles et al. 2003*). The highest weight recorded was 248.0 g (Niles et al. 2003*). Robinson et al. (2003*) suggested that arrival of knots appears to occur in 2 distinct periods: between 6 and

10 May and between 20 and 24 May. Most of the red knots captured over the entire period were adults (Robinson et al. 2003*). Although weight was correlated to body size, no systematic patterns of differential sizes in catches on different dates were evident (Robinson et al. 2003*). However, significant ($\square$ < 0.0001), but slight, differences in wing lengths were found between sides of the bay, years, date within years. When size and date were included, sub-adult knot weights did not differ from adult weights (Robinson et al. 2003*).

Robinson et al. (2003*) reported that weights of knots were relatively static until 11 May, after which average weight increased by 70.3 ± 3.6 g. In general, weight gain followed a logistic growth pattern, and knots that initially arrived in the first period had gained weight when they were re-captured during the second period (Robinson et al. 2003*). Niles et al. (2003*) found that year, day, and a year-day interaction were significant predictors of crude rate of mass gain in knots (reduced model, $\square^2$ = 0.24), and that body size, holding time, and time of day were also significant ($\square$ < 0.02) predictors (full model, R^2 = 0.29). Crude rate of mass gain was 5.22 g/day over all years, and a significant year*day interaction was caused by a decline from 8.5 g/day in 1997 to 2.3 g/day in 2002. Netting operations in 1997, however, began late on 22 May. Significant year effects ($\square$ = 0.0375) on knot crude rate of mass gain remained after accounting for proportion of the peak aerial survey count, and the regression of year and residuals from the previous regression (crude rate of mass - newly arrived birds) was negative and significant ($\square$ <0.0037). Weekly counts from aerial surveys are provided in Table 11.3. Mean mass of all species varied between states (P < 0.0001) and was generally higher in New Jersey. Although crude rate of mass gain declined in both states, the slope was somewhat steeper in Delaware, due to captures in 1997 ($\square$ = 0.044, year*state interaction; Niles et al. 2003*). Decreases in weight gain through the years were not monotonic (Table 11.4).

Using the initial weight distribution and the mean of weight change, Robinson et al. (2003*) derived an expected distribution of weights for any given day (assuming growth is deterministic and constant among years). Following this method, there was no evidence that growth rates varied among years (Robinson et al. 2003*). Comparison of these predicted distributions with actual catch data indicates the presence of several cohorts in the catch. The relative number of knots weighing less than would be expected after 11 May has increased over time, and suggests more birds are arriving later (Robinson et al. 2003*). Knots arriving late can gain weight at a faster rate (≤10 g/day; Robinson et al. 2003*). For 125 knots re-trapped within the same season, change in weight did not differ among years. Knots appear to be arriving later in Delaware Bay, and, in 2001 and 2002, second-arriving cohorts were 10 g lighter than earlier-arriving cohorts. Birds arriving by 16 May are predicted to reach target weight of 180 g by 28 May; those arriving after this date do not appear to do so (Robinson et al. 2003*).

Differences in the results of these analyses have generated 2 possible hypotheses: 1) horseshoe crab eggs do not exist in sufficient amounts to enable knots to reach migration threshold weights, or 2) knots are arriving later in May and do not reach threshold weights. The late arrival hypothesis (2) is supported by the change in distribution of weights through the season among years, the lack of a year effect on weight gain in same-season re-trapped birds, and weight gains of knots are similar among different capture sites in Delaware Bay. Hypothesis 2 is countered by no shift in timing of knot counts on aerial surveys, no general change in the timing of color-band re-sightings, and that predicted distributions consistently overestimate actual numbers of high-weight birds and under-estimate actual numbers of low-weight birds. Specific information on arrival of individually marked birds is needed to support or refute the arrival hypothesis, and much more information is needed on the condition of birds when they leave South America bound for Delaware Bay.

11.4.3. Red knot departure weights in Delaware Bay

Niles et al. (2003*) found that mean knot departure weights ranged from 26% to 51% above lean body mass. Baker et al. (2003) used logistic regression (0,1 if birds were in weight category by date) to determine the predicted percentage of knots in 4 mass categories ($\geq$160g, $\geq$180g, $\geq$190g, $\geq$200g) on 28 May from 1997 to 2002. The percentage of knots reaching 200 g on 28 May declined from 33.0% (1997) and 30.9% (1998) to 11.9% (2000) and 7.2% (2002). The same trend was detected in the most poorly-conditioned half of the population on 26 May (-20.5 g, t-test, P < 0.001), and a similar decreasing pattern existed for all weight categories (Baker et al. 2003). For all birds combined, percentages of individuals reaching departure mass (180 g) decreased significantly for knots from 1997 to 2002 (34.5% to 7.1%, logistic regression, Wald χ^2 = 206, $\square$ < 0.0001; Niles et al. 2003*). Weight gains in knots banded in previous years, during the last 5 days before departure (23–28 May), were variable among years (1997 - 2001): 10.4 g/day, 5.8 g/day, 2.6 g/day, 4.6 g/day, and 6.4 g/day. Despite a faster weight gain in late-arriving birds, Robinson et al. (2003*) found that only 42% of birds arriving on 20 May 2002 achieved target departure weight (180 g) by 28 May 2002 and only 84% of the more earlier arriving cohort reached target weight (vs. 95% in 1998). That fewer red knots are reaching migration threshold weights by the end of May in Delaware Bay is consistent among all analytical approaches.

11.5. Weights and Weight Gain in Ruddy Turnstones and Sanderlings

Niles et al. (2003*) found that ruddy turnstone arrival mass varied between 94.6 ± 8.6 and 98.6 ± 15.5 g, which was 6.1–9.9% below lean body mass (105 g). Arrival mass of sanderlings (49.6 ± 4.6), however, was closer their lean body mass (52 g) than either red knots or turnstones. Virtually all turnstones and sanderlings captured (>98%) were adults (Robinson et al. 2003*). Ruddy turnstones and sanderlings followed a similar weight gain schedule as knots (Robinson et al. 2003*). Relative to their arrival weights, turnstones increase their weight by 55%, at a rate of 7.2 ± 1.1 g/day and sanderlings by 70% (4.5 ± 1.3 g/day). Mean departure weight increases over lean body mass ranged from 46% to 52% for turnstones, and 48% to 80% for sanderlings (Robinson et al. 2003*). Year, day, and a year*day interaction, along with holding time and time of day, were significant predictors ($\square$ < 0.001) of crude rate of mass gain in turnstones (full model, R^2 = 0.42; Niles et al. 2003*). The crude rate of mass gain in ruddy turnstones only slightly declined over the period (0.5 g/day difference among years), and arriving birds did not significantly influence the crude rate of mass gain (Niles et al. 2003*). Analysis of individually re-trapped turnstones indicated a significant difference in weight gain among years (χ^2 = 10.82,

$\square = 0.029$), but there was no consistent trend across years and differences between years were <10% (Robertson et al. 2003*). Proportions of ruddy turnstones reaching departure mass (150 g) declined slightly for turnstones between 1997 and 2002 (logistic regression, Wald $\chi^2 = 206$, $\square <$ 0.025; Niles et al. 2003*). No trends were apparent in sanderlings for crude rate of mass gain, mass gain of re-trapped birds, or proportion of individuals reaching departure mass. Differences between states were minor for ruddy turnstones and absent for sanderlings. Because ruddy turnstones can dig for horseshoe crab eggs and sanderlings feed on a variety of invertebrates, they should be less sensitive than red knots to changes in surface egg density.

11.6. Weights and Weight Gain in Semipalmated and Least Sandpipers

Mizrahi (2002*) captured and weighed semipalmated and least sandpipers in Delaware Bay, between 1996 and 2002, to determine daily rates of fat or mass gain, the energetic condition of sandpipers, and whether these indices have changed since 1996. Least sandpipers migrate earlier in May through Delaware Bay and are primarily found in marshes, whereas semipalmated sandpipers are more dependent on horseshoe crab eggs for feeding and migration phenology. Sandpipers were captured at Thompson's Beach (1996, 1997, 2000, 2001, 2002) and Raybins Beach (1996, 2000, 2002). Between 1997 and 2001, ≥90,000 horseshoe crabs were annually harvested at Thompson's Beach; harvest was minimal before 1996 and the beach was closed to harvest in 2002. However, harvest did occur at nearby areas. Thompson's Beach is mainly used by species that forage on mudflats. Energetic condition of semipalmated sandpipers (fat mass) was estimated using a published regression model, and of least sandpipers by a published index that adjusted body mass for individual size. Linear regression was used to determine the relationship between date (starting 17 May for semipalmated and 8 May for least) and energetic condition; only days with ≥ 6 captures were included in the analysis. Analyses were conducted in 2 spatial groups (Thompson's Beach and Thompson's/Raybins combined) and in 2 time periods (all days and maximum mass gain period). Visual examination of residuals was made to ensure linear, parametric model assumptions were met. Effects of year were tested using an analysis of covariance. Significance of among-year comparisons was calculated with the Bonferroni adjustment.

Analysis of covariance showed highly significant year and date effects ($P \leq 0.001$) in semipalmated sandpipers for all days and for the period of maximum weight gains. Additionally, the interaction of date*year was highly significant ($P \leq 0.0001$), suggesting among year differences in daily fat mass gain. Fat mass gain in 1996 for combined Thompson's/Raybins cohorts (0.93–1.18 g/day, depending on analysis) was significantly greater compared to other years (0.41–0.45 g/day, averaged across years), which generally showed no among-year differences. Similarly, mean cohort fat mass was significantly greater in 1996 (8.77–9.97 g, depending on analysis) compared to other years (6.84–7.04 g depending on analysis, averaged across years) which showed no among-year differences. However, data from Thompson Beach alone showed more variability among years. In 1996, fat mass gain rate was 1.14–1.18 g/day (all days analysis and maximum mass gain period). By 2000, fat mass gain rates had declined to 0.18 g/day, and in 2002, the rate decreased to 0.08 g/day. No significant year effect or year-date interactions were found in least sandpipers, suggesting that rates of energy accumulation did not change significantly among years. Thus, semipalmated sandpipers showed a marked ($\approx 50\%$) and significant decrease in rates of energy accumulation from 1997–2002 relative to 1996, and, depending on year or analysis category, annual mean fat mass declined 8–41% compared to 1996. However, no significant change in rates of energy accumulation in least sandpipers was evident between 1996 and 2002, and mean energy condition varied only 4–10% among years. Differences between these congenerics may be attributable to differences in migration phenology and foraging ecology during spring stopovers in Delaware Bay.

12.0. RED KNOT SURVIVAL AND PRODUCTIVITY

12.1. Re-sighting Rates of Knots Banded in Florida and Argentina

Harrington et al. (1988) compared re-sighting rates of red knots wintering in Patagonia and Florida. Between 1980 and 1986, they banded 3,316 knots in Massachusetts, New Jersey, Florida, and Argentina. Of 309,013 knots scanned over a 5-year period, 1,730 flagged birds were re-sighted. After each site-year visit, re-sighting rate for each band class was calculated as: [(number re-sighted $\div$ number banded) $\div$ number scanned]. The $\log_2$ of re-sighting rate was regressed against time since banding, and site-specific regression slopes were compared to determine location effect. Regression slopes (β) were used to determine annual re-sighting rate (sensu Caughley 1977) as: $p_s = e^{12\beta}$. Relative to Florida (3.04%, $n = 263$ marked), a significantly higher percentage ($\chi^2 = 16.7$, $\square < 0.01$) of red knots banded in Argentina (13.8%, $n = 181$ marked) were re-sighting in New Jersey or Massachusetts. No birds banded in either Argentina or Florida were found at the opposite site. Although these wintering populations appear discrete, wing and bill lengths of birds captured at each site did not differ (ANOVA, $\square > 0.05$). Slopes of regression of $\log_2$ re-sighting rate vs. time since banding were significantly different (ANOVA, $\square = 0.014$). The difference was due to Florida; slopes for Massachusetts and New Jersey did not differ ($\square = 0.865$). Re-sighting rate of birds wintering in Florida ($p_s = 0.758$, $\beta = -0.023$, $\square^2 = 0.692$, $\square = 0.020$) was twice that of birds wintering in Argentina (New Jersey: $p_s = 0.340$, $\beta = -0.089$, $\square^2 = 0.691$, $\square = 0.011$; Massachusetts: $p_s = 0.358$, $\beta = -0.0855$, $\square^2 = 0.810$, $\square = 0.0001$). Because of similar re-sighting rates between New Jersey and Massachusetts, evidence suggests that knots are site faithful during migration. Age structure should not influence differences in Florida birds after the first re-sighting year. Low re-sighting rates could be due to some band loss in the population.

12.2. Survival Rate

To determine effects of reduced departure mass on return rate, Baker at al. (2003) analyzed return rates of adults relative to capture mass and mark-recapture data from catches. Red knots known to survive ≥ 1 year after capture had a heavier initial capture weight than birds that were not re-sighted (ANOVA, $\square = 13.8$, $\square < 0.001$), which suggests that knots arriving earlier in May should have more time to gain weight and enhance survival. However, known survivors captured during the peak of migration 15–30 May ($n = 383$, mass of birds set on 23 May) showed a decline in predicted departure mass on 28 May in recent years. Observed mass on 23 May was calculated by fitting a log-link General Linearized Model of known survivor weights with date and year as covariates. Median dates of capture of known survivors did not change among years (Kruskal-Wallis, $H = 4.163$, $\square = 0.329$). Mark-recapture analysis was restricted to re-sighting of knots flagged in either Tierra del Fuego or southern Brazil. The program U-care confirmed that Cormack-Jolly-Seber assumptions estimators were met, and program MARK (2.1) was used to estimate survival rates (for 3-year periods). Although annual survival tended to decline from 86.7% (1994/95–1997/98) to 53.9% (1998/99–2000/01), 95% confidence limits (determined from profile likelihood; 0.54–1.00, 0.45–0.633) overlapped among these periods. An estimate for 2001/02 was highly variable (0.49–1.00, 95% confidence limit; Baker et al. 2003). During a population decline of *islandica* knots in Britain, annual adult survival was only 76%, whereas annual adult survival was 80% when the population was stable (Boyd and Piersma 2001). Confidence limits during 1998/99–2000/01 were well below the mean adult survival Britain-wintering knots. Greater effort to re-sight and recapture marked birds would improve the ability to estimate and interpret survival rate data. Inscribed color flags have been suggested as a way to increase accuracy and ease of identifying individuals scanned from flocks (Atkinson et al. 2003).

12.3. Population Projections

Baker et al. (2003) constructed a matrix model to evaluate demographic effects of current vital rates. No information exists for juvenile survival of *ru⊡a* red knots, but is about 25% of adult survival in *islandica* knots (Boyd and Piersma 2001). Similarly, no information exists on knot fecundity. If juvenile survival is 50% of adult survival in the best years (87.6%), and fecundity is uniformly distributed with a mean of 0.29 (maximum = 0.58, minimum = 0.0), then the Tierra del Fuego population is estimated to be stable at about 70,000 birds. If adult survival continues at the lower level (53.9%), the population is predicted to be extinct or nearly so by 2010. No probabilities of extinction at different adult survival rates, however, were provided in the analysis. Aerial counts made in Tierra del Fuego in 2003 were slightly higher than counts made in 2002 (R. I. G. Morrison, personal communication) and suggest that probability of extinction by 2010 is likely low.

12.4. Juvenile Age Ratios

Based on observations of wintering and early spring flocks of red knots, Baker et al. (2003) reported that the percentage of juveniles in captures made in Tierra del Fuego has gradually declined from 19% in 1995 (Rio Grande, $n \approx 500$ knots) to 16% in 2000 (Rio Grande, $n \approx 500$) to 10% in 2001 (Rio Grande, $n \approx 500$), 6% in 2002 (Bahía Lomas, $n = 231$), and 5% in 2003 (Bahía Lomas, $n = 200$). In 1995, the percentage of immature knots was much lower in catches northward of Tierra del Fuego in Rio Grande at Punta Rasa, Argentina (8%, $n = 66$), and Lagoa do Peixe, Brazil (4.6%, $n = 394$). The mean percentage of juvenile *islandica* knots wintering in Britain ranged from 29% in years of increasing numbers to 14% in stable years to 12% in years of decreasing numbers (Boyd and Piersma 2001). Recent estimates from Tierra del Fuego are well below even the mean of the worst years in Britain. For 21 years when >50 knots were captured at Ottenby, Sweden, the proportion of juveniles was 37.4% and ranged from 0 to 95%. The percentages of juveniles in catches of red knots in Australia, the southern migration terminus of □ □ *C. rogersi*, varied 3–14% (northwest) and 3–69% (southeast; Minton et al. 2002*). Neither site had sequential years at low levels. Successive years of poor recruitment would certainly contribute to population declines.

13.0. LITERATURE CITED

(* indicate unpublished reports, submitted manuscripts, or abstracts)

Andres, B. A. 1999. Effects of persistent shoreline oil on breeding success and chick growth in black oystercatchers. Auk 116:640–650.

*Alemany, D., E. Ieno, D. Blanco, and R. Bastida. 2001. Red knot diet and prey size selection during northward migration at Punta Rasa, Buenos Aires, Argentina. Wader Study Group Bulletin 95:17–18 (abstract).

*Atkinson, P. W., N. A. Clark, and R. A. Robinson. 2003. Survival Rates and Body Condition of red Knots in Delaware Bay—Influence of Body Condition at Departure on Survival, Chapter 1. British Trust for Ornithology Research Report No. 308, Thetford, Norfolk, United Kingdom. 41 pp.

*Atlantic States Marine Fisheries Commission. 1998a. Interstate fishery management plan for the horseshoe crab. Fishery Management Report No. 32, Washington, D. C. 50 pp.

*Atlantic States Marine Fisheries Commission. 1998b. Terms of reference and advisory report for the horseshoe crab stock assessment peer review. Stock Assessment Report No. 98-01, Washington, D. C. 13 pp.

*Atlantic States Marine Fisheries Commission. 1998c. Horseshoe crab stock assessment report for peer review. Stock Assessment Report No. 98-01 (Supplement), Washington, D. C. 43 pp.

*Atlantic States Marine Fisheries Commission. 2000. Addendum I to the Fishery Management Plan for Horseshoe Crab. Fishery Management Report No. 32a, Washington, D. C. 9 pp.

*Atlantic States Marine Fisheries Commission. 2001. Addendum II to the Fishery Management Plan for Horseshoe Crab. Fishery Management Report No. 32a, Washington, D. C. 5 pp.

*Aubry, Y., and R. Cotter. 2001. Using trend information to develop the Quebec shorebird conservation plan. Canadian Wildlife Service Bird Trends 8:21–25.

Baker, A. J., P. M. Gonzalez, L. J. Niles, T. Piersma, I. L. S. Nascimento, P. W. Atkinson, N. A. Clark, C. D. T. Minton, M. Peck, H. Sitters, and G. Aarts. 2003. Rapid population decline in red knots ☐*alidris canutus ru*☐*a* since 2000: fitness consequences of late arrival and decreased refueling rates in Delaware Bay. Science 299: *in* ☐*ress*.

Baker, A. J., P. M. Gonzalez, T. Piersma, C. D. T. Minton, J. R. Wilson, H. Sitters, D. Graham, R. Jessop, P. Collins, P. de Goeji, M. K. Peck, R. Lini, L. Bala, G. Pagnoni, A. Vila, E. Bremer, R. Bastida, E. Ieno, D. Blanco, S. de Lima, I. Do Nascimento, S. S. Scherer, M. P. Schneider, A. Silva, and A. A. F. Rodrigues. 1998. Northbound migration of red knots ☐*alidris canutus ru*☐*a* in Argentina and Brazil: report on results obtained by an international expedition in March and April 1997. Wader Study Group Bulletin 88:64–75.

*Bart, J. R., S. Brown, R. I. G. Morrison, and B. A. Harrington. 2003. Population trends of North American shorebirds. Auk 119: *sub*☐*itted*

*Below, T. H. 2001. Red knot monitoring in southwest Florida. Wader Study Bulletin 95: 11–12 (abstract).

Berkson, J., and C. N. Shuster, Jr. 1999. The horseshoe crab: the battle for a true multiple-use resource. Fisheries 24:6–10

Blomqvist, S., N. Holmgren, S. Åkesson, A. Hedenström, and J. Pettersson. 2002. Indirect effects of lemming cycles on sandpiper dynamics: 50 years of counts from southern Sweden. Oecologia 133:146-158.

Botton, M. L. 1984. Effects of laughing gull and shorebird predation on the intertidal fauna at Cape May, New Jersey. Estuarine, Coastal and Shelf Science 18:209–220.

Botton, M. L. 1993. Predation by herring gulls and great black-backed gulls on horseshoe crabs. Wilson Bulletin 105:518–521.

Botton, M. L. 2000. Toxicity of cadmium and mercury to horseshoe crab (☐*i*☐*ulus* ☐*oly*☐*he*☐*us*) embryos and larvae. Bulletin of Environmental Contaminants and Toxicology 64:137–143.

Botton, M. L., K. Johnson, and L. Helleby. 1998. Effects of copper and zinc on embryos and larvae of the horseshoe crab, ☐*i*☐*ulus* ☐*oly*☐*he*☐*us*. Archives of Environmental Contamination and Toxicology 64:25–32.

Botton, M.L., R.E. Loveland, and T.R. Jacobsen. 1988. Beach erosion and geochemical factors: influence on spawning success of horseshoe crabs (□i□ulus □oly□he□us) in Delaware Bay. Marine Biology 99:325–332.

Botton, M. L., R. E. Loveland, and T. R. Jacobsen. 1994. Site selection by migratory shorebirds in Delaware Bay, and its relationship to beach characteristics and abundance of horseshoe crab (□i□ulus □oly□he□us) eggs. Auk 111:605–616.

Botton, M. L., and J. W. Ropes. 1987. Populations of horseshoe crabs, □i□ulus □oly□he□us, on the northwestern Atlantic continental shelf. Fisheries Bulletin 85:805–812.

Boyd, H. 1992. Arctic summer conditions and British knot numbers: an exploratory analysis. Wader Study Group Bulletin 64 (supplement):144–152.

Boyd, H., and T. Piersma. 2001. Changing balance between survival and recruitment explains population trends in red knots Calidris canutus islandica wintering in Britain, 1969–1995. Ardea 89:301–317.

Brayton, A. F., and D. C. Schneider. 2000. Shorebird abundance and invertebrate density during the boreal winter and spring at Peninsula Valdez, Argentina. Waterbirds 23:277–282.

*Brousseau, L .J., M. Sclafani, D. R. Smith and D. B. Carter. 2002. Acoustic and radio tracking of horseshoe crabs (□i□ulus □oly□he□us) to assess foreshore and subtidal habitat use in Delaware Bay. Annual Meeting of the American Fisheries Society, Baltimore, Maryland (poster).

*Brown, S., C. Hickey, B. Harrington, and R. Gill (editors). 2001. The U. S. shorebird conservation plan, second edition. Manomet Center for Conservation Sciences. Manomet, Massachusetts. 60 pp.

Buckel, J. A., and K. A. McKown. 2002. Competition between juvenile striped bass and bluefush: resource partitioning and growth rate. Marine Ecology Progress Series 234:191–204

Buhl-Mortensen, L., and S. Welin. 1998. The ethics of doing relevant science: the precautionary principle and the significance of non-significant results. Science and Engineering Ethics 4:401–412.

Burger, J. 1981. The effect of human activity on birds at a coastal bay. Biological Conservation 21:231–241.

Burger, J. 1997. Heavy metals in the eggs and muscle of horseshoe crabs (□i□ulus □oly□he□us) from Delaware Bay. Environmental Monitoring and Assessment 46:279–287.

Burger, J., D. Caldwell Hahn, and J. Chase. 1979. Aggressive interactions in mixed-species flocks of migrating shorebirds. Animal Behaviour 27:459–469.

Burger, J., C. Dixon, T. Shukla, N. Tsipoura, and M. Gochfeld. 2002a. Metal Levels in Horseshoe Crabs (□i□ulus □oly□he□us) from Maine to Florida. Environmental Research 90:227–236.

Burger, J., C. Dixon, T. Shukla, N. Tsipoura, H. Jensen, M. Fitzgerald, R. Ramos and M. Gochfeld. 2002b. Metals in Horseshoe Crabs from Delaware Bay. Archives of Environmental Contaminants and Toxicology 44:36–42.

Burger, J., and M. Gochfeld. 1991. Human activity influence and diurnal and nocturnal foraging of sanderlings (□alidris alba). Condor 93:259–265.

*Burger J., C. Jeitner, and S. Carlucci. 2003. Foraging behavior of shorebirds and gulls at a migratory stopover in Delaware Bay. Unpublished report, Nelson Biology Laboratory, Rutgers University, Piscataway, New Jersey.

Burger, J., L. Niles, and K. E. Clark. 1997. Importance of beach, mudflat, and marsh habitats to migrant shorebirds on Delaware Bay. Biological Conservation 79:283–292.

Burger, J., S. Seyboldt, N. Morganstein, and K. Clark. 1993. Heavy metals and selenium in feathers of three shorebird species from Delaware Bay. Environmental Monitoring and Assessment 28:189–198.

*Carter, D. 2002. Preliminary analysis of red knot and turnstone concentration areas in Delaware 1997–2000. Unpublished report, Delaware Coastal Management Programs, Dover, Delaware.

*Carter, D. B., N. A. Clark, and J. D. Hewes (editors). 2002. Delaware Bay – 2000/2001 the Delaware shorebird monitoring team bi-annual report. Unpublished report, Delaware Coastal Management Programs, Dover, Delaware.

*Carter, D., and R. R. Scarborough. 2002. Local wind direction and intensity as a major factor for habitat preference and utilization by red knot on Delaware Bay during spring migration. Unpublished report, Delaware Coastal Management Programs, Dover, Delaware.

Castro, G., and J. P. Myers. 1988. A statistical method to estimate the cost of flight in birds. Journal Field Ornithology 59:369–38

Castro, G., and J. P. Myers. 1989. Flight range estimates for shorebirds. Auk 106:474–476.

Castro, G., J. P. Myers, and A. R. Place. 1989. Assimilation efficiency of sanderlings (□*alidris alba*) feeding on horseshoe crab (□*i*□*ulus* □*oly*□*he*□*us*) eggs. Physiological Zoology 62:716–731.

Castro, G., J. P. Myers, and R. E. Ricklefs. 1992. Ecology and energetics of sanderlings migrating to four latitudes. Ecology 73:833–844.

Castro, G., and J. P. Myers. 1993. Shorebird predation on eggs of horseshoe crabs during spring stopover on Delaware Bay. Auk 110:927–930.

Caughley, G. 1977. Analysis of vertebrate populations. John Wiley & Sons, New York, New York. 244 pp.

Clark, K. E., L. J. Niles, and J. Burger. 1993. Abundance and distribution of migrant shorebirds in Delaware Bay. Condor 95:694–705.

*Clark, K. E. and L. J. Niles (editors). 2000. Northern Atlantic regional shorebird plan, version 1.0. Unpublished report, New Jersey Endangered and Nongame Species Program, Division of Wildlife, Trenton, New Jersey (available at <http://shorebirdplan.fws.gov>).

Cooper, J. M. 1994. Least sandpiper (□*alidris* □*inutila*). Pages 1–28 *in* A. Poole and F. Gill, editors. The birds of North America, No. 115. Academy of Natural Sciences, Philadelphia, and The American Ornithologists' Union, Washington D. C.

Davidson, N. C., and P. I. Rothwell. 1993. Disturbance to waterfowl on estuaries: the conservation and coastal management implications of current knowledge. Wader Study Group Bulletin 68:97–105.

*Escudero, G., and L. J. Niles. 2001. Are there alternative food resources for knots in Delaware Bay? Wader Study Group Bulletin 95:13 (abstract).

*Eubanks, T. L., J. R. Stoll, and P. Kerlinger. 2000. The economic impact of tourism based on horseshoe crab-shorebird migration in New Jersey. Unpublished Report, Fermata, Inc., Austin, Texas. 91 pp.

*Eyler S., and M. Millard. 2002. Spawning frequency and beach fidelity of horseshoe crabs in Delaware Bay. Annual Meeting of the American Fisheries Society, Baltimore, Maryland (poster).

*Falkingham, J. C., R. Chagnon, and S. McCourt. 2001. Sea ice in the Canadian arctic in the 21st century, chapter II:12. The state of the arctic cryosphere during the extreme warm summer of 1998: documenting cryospheric variability in the Canadian arctic. Final report, CCAF summer 1998 project team, Environment Canada (available at <http://www.socc.ca>).

Figuerola, J. 1999. Effects of salinity on rates of infestation of waterbirds by haematozoa. Ecography 22: 681-685.

Galbraith, H., R. Jones, R. Park, J. Clough, S. Herrod-Julius, B. Harrington, and G. Page. 2002. Global climate change and sea level rise: potential losses of intertidal habitat for shorebirds. Waterbirds 25: 173–183.

Gill, J. A., K. Norris, and W. J. Sutherland. 2001. Why behavioural responses may not reflect the population consequences of human disturbance. Biological Conservation 97:265–268.

Gill, R. E., Jr., P. Canevari, and E. H. Iversen. 1998. Eskimo curlew (□u□enius borealis). Pages 1–28 in A. Poole and F. Gill, editors. The birds of North America, No. 347. Academy of Natural Sciences, Philadelphia, and The American Ornithologists' Union, Washington D. C.

*Gillings, S. 2002. What is the rate of weight loss between capture and weighing for red knots processed in Delaware and New Jersey in May 1998, 1999, and 2000 and how do weights change through migration. Unpublished report, Delaware Coastal Management Programs, Dover, Delaware.

*Galofre, J. 2002. Beach nourishment analysis of Delaware Bay beaches in Delaware state and applications to coastal management. Unpublished report, Delaware Department of Natural Resources and Environmental Control. Dover, Delaware.

González, P. M., T. Piersma, and Y. Verkuil. 1996. Food, feeding, and refueling of red knots during northward migration at San Antonio Oeste, Rio Negro, Argentina. Journal of Field Ornithology 67:575–591.

*González, P. M., D. Price, and G. Morrison. 2001. Migration of knots through Bahía de San Antonio, Río Negro, Argentina. Wader Study Group Bulletin 95:11 (abstract).

Goss-Custard, J. D. and N. Verboven. 1993. Disturbance and feeding shorebirds on the Exe estuary. Wader Study Group Bulletin 68:59–66.

Gratto-Trevor, C. L. 1992. Semipalmated sandpiper (□alidris □usilla). Pages 1–20 in A. Poole and F. Gill, editors. The birds of North America, No. 6. Academy of Natural Sciences, Philadelphia, and The American Ornithologists' Union, Washington D. C.

Gretton, A. 1991. Conservation of the Slender-billed Curlew. International Council for Bird Preservation Monograph No. 6, Cambridge, England. 159 pp.

Gudmundsson, G. A., Å. Lindström, and T. Alerstam. 1991. Optimal fat loads and long-distance flights by migrating knots (□*alidris canutus*), sanderlings (□□*alba*), and turnstones (□*renaria inter*□*res*). Ibis 133:140–152.

*Haramis, G. M., M. A. Teece, and D. B. Carter. 2002. Use of stable isotopes to determine the relative importance of horseshoe crab eggs in the diet of long-distance migrant shorebirds in Delaware Bay. Unpublished report, Delaware Coastal Management Programs, Dover, Delaware.

Harrington, B. A. 2001. Red knot (□*alidris canutus*). Pages 1–32 *in* A. Poole and F. Gill, editors. The birds of North America, No. 563. Academy of Natural Sciences, Philadelphia, and The American Ornithologists' Union, Washington D. C.

*Harrington, B. A. 2002. Shorebird migration on Delaware Bay – Pondering the numbers. Unpublished report, Manomet Center for Conservation Sciences, Manomet, Massachusetts.

Harrington, B. A., P. de T. Z. Antas, and F. Silva. 1986. Northward shorebird migration on the Atlantic coast of southern Brazil. Vida Silvestre Neotropical 1:45–54.

*Harrington, B., and N. Drilling. 1996. Investigations of effects of disturbance to migratory shorebirds at migration stopover sites on the U. S. Atlantic coast. Unpublished report, Manomet Center for Conservation Sciences, Manomet, Massachusetts.

Harrington, B. A., J. A. Hagan, and L. E. Leddy. 1988. Site fidelity and survival differences between two groups of New World red knots (□*alidris canutus*). Auk 88:439–445.

Harrington, B. A., and R. I. G. Morrison. 1979. Semipalmated sandpiper migration in North America. Studies in Avian Biology 2:83-100.

*Harrington, B. A., and B. Winn. 2001. Red knots of southeastern United States: A preliminary report of recent investigations into the insular qualities of the population. Wader Study Group Bulletin 95:12 (abstract).

Helmers, D. L. 1992. Shorebird Management Manual. Western Hemisphere Shorebird Reserve Network, Manomet Center for Conservation Sciences, Manomet, Massachusetts. 58 pp.

Hicklin, P. W. 1987. The migration of shorebirds in the Bay of Fundy. Wilson Bulletin 99:540–570.

Hitchcock, C. L., and C. Gratto-Trevor. 1997. Diagnosing a shorebird local population decline with a stage-structured population model. Ecology 78:522–534.

Hockin, D., M. Ounsted, M. Gorman, D. Hill, V. Keller, and M. A. Barker. 1992. Examination of the effects of disturbance on birds with reference to its importance in ecological assessments. Journal of Environmental Management 36:253–286.

Hollander M., and D. A. Wolfe. 1973. Non-parametric statistical methods. John Wiley & Sons, Inc. New York, New York. 503 pp.

Howe, M. A., P. H. Geissler, and B. A. Harrington. 1989. Population trends of North American shorebirds based on the International Shorebird Survey. Biological Conservation 49:185–199.

Itow, T., T. Igarashi, R. E. Loveland, and M. L. Botton. 1998a. Heavy metals inhibit limb regeneration in horseshoe crab larvae. Archives of Environmental Contamination and Toxicology 35:457–463.

Itow, T., R. E. Loveland, and M. L. Botton. 1998b. Developmental abnormalities in horseshoe crab embryos caused by exposure to heavy metals. Archives of Environmental Contamination and Toxicology 35:33–40.

Jehl, J. R. Jr., J. Klima, and R. E. Harris. 2001. Short-billed dowitcher (□i□nodro□us griseus). Pages 1–28 in A. Poole and F. Gill, editors. The birds of North America, No. 564. Academy of Natural Sciences, Philadelphia, and The American Ornithologists' Union, Washington D. C.

Kendeigh, S. C., V. R. Dolnick, and V. M. Gavrilov. 1977. Avian energetics. Pages 127–204 in J. Pinowski and S. C. Kendeigh, editors. Granivorous birds in ecosystems. Cambridge University Press, New York, New York. 431 pp.

Kersten, M., and T. Piersma. 1987. High levels of energy expenditure in shorebirds: metabolic adaptations to an energetically expensive way of life. Ardea 75:175–187

Koolhaas, A., A. Dekinga, and T. Piersma. 1993. Disturbance of foraging Knots by aircraft in the Dutch Wadden Sea in August-October 1992. Wader Study Group Bulletin 68:20–22.

Kraeuter, J. N., and S. R. Fegley. 1994. Vertical disturbance of sediments by horseshoe crabs (□i□ulus □oly□he□us) during their spawning season. Estuaries 17:288–294.

Kvist, A., Å. Lindström, M. Green, T. Piersma, G. H. Visser. 2001. Carrying large fuel loads during sustained flight is cheaper than expected. Nature 413:730–732.

Lafferty, K. D. 2001. Birds at a Southern California beach: seasonality, habitat use and disturbance by human activity. Biodiversity and Conservation 10:1949–1962.

Lindström, Å, and T. Piersma. 1993. Mass changes in migrating birds: the evidence for fat and protein storage re-examined. Ibis 135:70-78.

Lutcavage, M. 1981. The status of marine turtles in Chesapeake Bay and Virginia coastal waters. M. S. Thesis, College of William and Mary, Williamstown, Virginia. 126 pp.

Lutcavage, M., and J. A. Musick. 1985. Aspects of the biology of sea turtles in Virginia. Copeia 1985:449–456.

MacWhirter, B., P. Austin-Smith, Jr., and D. Kroodsma. 2002. Sanderling (□alidris alba). Pages 1–28 in A. Poole and F. Gill, editors. The birds of North America, No. 653. Academy of Natural Sciences, Philadelphia, and The American Ornithologists' Union, Washington D. C.

Madsen, J. 1998. Experimental refuges for migratory waterfowl in Danish wetlands: I. Baseline assessment of the disturbance effects of recreational activities. Journal of Applied Ecology 35:386–397.

*Maghini, M. K. R. 1996. Availability of contaminants to migratory shorebirds consuming horseshoe crab eggs on Delaware Bay beaches. Unpublished report, No. CBFO-C96-02, U. S. Fish and Wildlife Service, Chesapeake Bay Field Office, Annapolis, Maryland.

*Manion, M. M., R. A. West, and R. E. Unsworth. 2000. Economic assessment of the Atlantic coast horseshoe crab fishery. Unpublished report, U. S. Fish and Wildlife Service, Division of Economics, Arlington, Virginia.

*Meyer, S. R., J. Burger, and L. J. Niles. ND. Habitat use, spatial dynamics, and stopover ecology of red knots on Delaware Bay. Unpublished report, New Jersey Endangered and Nongame Species Program, Division of Wildlife, Trenton, New Jersey. 31 pp.

*Millard, M. J., D. R. Smith, S. Michels, J. Brust, and J. Berkson. 2000. Stock assessment of Atlantic coast horseshoe crabs: a proposed framework. Unpublished report, Atlantic States Marine Fisheries Commission, Washington, D. C.

*Minton, C., R. Jessop, P. Collins, and C. Hassell. 2002. Year 2001 Arctic breeding success, as measured by the percentages of first year birds in wader populations in Australia in the 2001/02 Austral summer. Arctic Birds, Newsletter of the International Breeding Conditions Survey, International Wader Study Group.

Mizrahi, D. S. 1999. Migratory behavior and ecophysiology of Semipalmated Sandpipers during spring migration stopover. Ph. D. dissertation. Clemson University, Clemson, South Carolina.

*Mizrahi, D. S. 2002. Mass gain and stopover length in semipalmated and least sandpipers staging in Delaware Bay during spring migration. Unpublished report, New Jersey Audubon Society, Cape May Court House, New Jersey.

Mizrahi, D. S., R. L. Holberton, and S. A. Gauthreaux, Jr. 2000. Patterns of corticosterone secretion in Semipalmated Sandpipers at a major stopover site during spring migration. The Auk 118:79-91.

Morrison, R. I. G., R. E. Gill, Jr., B. A. Harrington, S. Skagen, G. W. Page, C. L. Gratto-Trevor, and S. M. Haig. 2001. Estimates of shorebird populations in North America. Occasional paper No. 104, Canadian Wildlife Service, Ottawa, Ontario. 64 pp.

Morrison, R. I. G., and B. A. Harrington. 1992. The migration system of the red knot □*alidris canutus ru*□*a* in the New World. Wader Study Group Bulletin 64 (supplement):71–84.

*Morrison, R. I. G., and P. Hicklin. 2001. Recent trends in shorebird populations in the Atlantic provinces. Canadian Wildlife Service Bird Trends 8:16–19.

Morrison, R. I. G., and R. K. Ross. 1989a. Atlas of nearctic shorebirds on the coast of South America, Volume 1. Canadian Wildlife Service, Ottawa, Ontario. 128 pp.

Morrison, R. I. G., and R. K. Ross. 1989b. Atlas of nearctic shorebirds on the coast of South America, Volume 2. Canadian Wildlife Service, Ottawa, Ontario. 325 pp.

Myers, J. P. 1983. Conservation of migrating shorebirds: staging areas, geographical bottlenecks, and regional movements. American Birds 37:23–25.

Myers, J. P. 1986. Sex and gluttony on Delaware Bay. Natural History 95:68–77.

*Nascimento, I. 2001. Migration and other biological data of □*alidris canutus ru*□*a* from Brazil. Wader Study Group Bulletin 95:11 (abstract).

*National Marine Fisheries Service. 2002. National Oceanic and Atmospheric Administration Fisheries 2001 Report. U.S. Department of Commerce, National Oceanic and Atmospheric Administration, National Marine Fisheries Service, Silver Spring, Maryland. 48 pp.

Nettleship, D. N. 2000. Ruddy Turnstone (☐renaria inter☐res). Pages 1–32 in A. Poole and F. Gill, editors. The birds of North America, No. 537. Academy of Natural Sciences, Philadelphia, and The American Ornithologists' Union, Washington, D. C.

*Niles, L. J., K. Clark, H. Sitters, C. Minton, A. Baker, A. Dey, N. Clark, D. Veitch, J. Burger. 2003. Trends in mass gain and abundance of Red Knot (☐alidris canutus ru☐a), Ruddy Turnstone (☐renaria inter☐res), and Sanderling (☐alidris alba) on Delaware Bay, USA. Condor 105: sub☐itted.

*Niles, L. W., M. Peck, and R. Lathrop. 2001. Breeding habitat of the red knot in Nunavut, Canada. Wader Study Group Bulletin 95:14 (abstract).

*Oring, L., B. Harrington, S. Brown, and C. Hickey (editors). 2000. National shorebird research needs: A proposal for a national research program and example high priority research topics. Unpublished report (see http://shorebirdplan.fws.gov).

Peterman, R. M., and M. M'Gonigle. 1992. Statistical power analysis and the precautionary principle. Marine Pollution Bulletin 24:231-234.

Pfister, C., B. A. Harrington, and M. Lavine. 1992. The impact of human disturbance on shorebirds at a migration staging area. Biological Conservation 60:115–126.

Pfister, C., M. J. Kasprzyk, and B. A. Harrington. 1998. Body-fat levels and annual return in migrating semipalmated sandpipers. Auk 115:904–915.

Piersma, T. 1996. Energetic constraints on the non-breeding distribution of coastal shorebirds. International Wader Studies 8:122–135.

Piersma, T. 1997. Do global patterns of habitat use and migration strategies co-evolve with relative investments in immunocompetence due to spatial variation in parasite pressure? Oikos 80: 623-631.

*Piersma, T. 2000. Energetics of body mass changes in red knots staging in Delaware Bay in May 1998. Unpublished report, Netherlands Institute for Sea Research, Trexel, The Netherlands.

Piersma, T., and A. J. Baker. 2000. Life history characteristics and the conservation of migratory shorebirds. Pages 105-124 in L. M. Gosling and W. J. Sutherland, editors. Behaviour and Conservation. Cambridge University Press, London, England. 438 pp.

Piersma, T., and N. Davidson (editors.). 1992. The migration of knots. Wader Study Group Bulletin 64 (supplement). 209 pp.

Piersma, T., A. Hedenstroem, J. H. Bruggemann. 1997. Climb and flight speeds of shorebirds embarking on an intercontinental flight; do they achieve the predicted optimal behaviour? Ibis 139:299-304.

Piersma T, G. A. Gudmunsson, and K. Lilliendahl. 1999. Rapid changes in the size of different functional organ and muscle groups during refueling in a long-distance migrating shorebird. Physiological Biochemical Zoology 72: 405–415.

Pooler, P. S., D. R. Smith, R. E. Loveland, M. L. Botton, and S. F. Michels. 2003. Assessment of sampling methods to estimate horseshoe crab (□i□ulus □oly□he□us) egg density in Delaware Bay. Fisheries Bulletin 101: *in* □ress.

Raveling, D. G., and E. A. Lefebvre. 1967. Energy metabolism and theoretical flight range of birds. Bird Banding 38:97–113.

*Robinson, R. A., P. W. Atkinson, and N. A. Clark. 2003. Arrival and weight gain of Red Knots, Ruddy Turnstones, and Sanderlings staging in Delaware Bay in spring. British Trust for Ornithology Research Report No. 307, Thetford, Norfolk, United Kingdom. 55 pp.

Rodgers Jr, J. A., and S. T. Schwikert. 2002. Buffer-zone distances to protect foraging and loafing waterbirds from disturbance by personal watercraft and outboard-powered boats. Conservation Biology 16:216–224.

Rodgers Jr, J. A., and H. T. Smith. 1997. Buffer zone distances to protect foraging and loafing waterbirds from human disturbance in Florida. Wildlife Society Bulletin 25:139–145.

Shuster, C. N., Jr. 1982. A pictorial review of the natural history and ecology of the horseshoe crab, □i□ulus □oly□he□us, with reference to other Limulidae. Pages 1-52 *in* J. Bonaventura, C. Bonaventura, and S. Tesh (editors). Physiology and biology of horseshoe crabs: studies on normal and environmentally stressed animals. Alan R. Liss, Inc., New York, New York.

*Shuster, C.N., Jr. 1996. The Delaware Bay area—an ideal habitat for horseshoe crabs. Unpublished report, Public Service Electric and Gas Company, Hancocks Bridge, New Jersey. 26 pp.

Shuster, C. N., Jr., and M. L. Botton. 1985. A contribution to the population biology of horseshoe crabs, □i□ulus □oly□he□us (L.), in Delaware Bay. Estuaries 8:363–372.

*Sitters, H. 2001. Behavioral evidence that shorebirds may suffer shortages of available horseshoe crabs' eggs in Delaware Bay. Wader Study Group Bulletin 95:14 (abstract).

Sitters, H. P., P. M. Gonzalez, T. Piersma, A. J. Baker, and D. J. Price. 2001. Day and night feeding habitat of red knots in Patagonia: Profitability versus safety. Journal of Field Ornithology 72:86–95.

Smit, C. J., and G. J. M. Visser. 1993. Effects of disturbance on shorebirds: a summary of existing knowledge from the Dutch Wadden Sea and Delta Area. Wader Study Group Bulletin 68:6–19.

*Smith, D. R., and S. Bennett. 2003. Horseshoe carb spawning activity in Delaware Bay: a preliminary report on 2002 and a comparison from 1999 to 2002. Unpublished report, U. S. Geological Survey, Kearnysville, West Virginia.

*Smith, D. R., N. Jackson, S. Love, K. Nordstrom, R. Weber, and D. Carter. 2002a. Beach nourishment on Delaware Bay beaches to restore habitat for horseshoe crab spawning and shorebird foraging. Unpublished report, The Nature Conservancy, Delaware Bayshores Office, Wilmington, Delaware. 51 pp.

Smith, D. R., P. S. Pooler, R. E. Loveland, M. L. Botton, S. F. Michels, R. G. Webber, and D. B. Carter. 2002b. Horseshoe crab (◻i◻ulus ◻oly◻he◻us) reproductive activity on Delaware Bay beaches: interactions with beach characteristics. Journal of Coastal Research 18: *in* ◻*ress*.

Smith, D. R., P. S. Pooler, B. L. Swan, S. Michels, W. R. Hall, P. Himachak, and M. J. Millard. 2002c. Spatial and temporal distribution of horseshoe crab (◻i◻ulus ◻oly◻he◻us) spawning in Delaware Bay: implications for monitoring. Estuaries 25:115–125.

Snedecor, G. W., and W. G. Cochran. 1980. Statistical methods, seventh edition. Iowa State University Press, Ames, Iowa. 507 pp.

*Southeastern Cooperative Wildlife Disease Study. 2002. Influenza viruses in gulls, terns, and shorebirds of the United States Atlantic and Gulf coasts. Unpublished report, University of Georgia, Athens, Georgia.

*Stillman, R. A., P. W. Atkinson, N. A. Clark, S. Gillings, I. G. Henderson, S. E. Love, R. A. Robinson, R. G. Weber, and S. L. Bardsley. 2003. Functional Responses of Shorebirds Feeding on Horseshoe Crab Eggs, Chapter 2. British Trust for Ornithology Research Report No. 308, Norfolk, United Kingdom. 41 pp.

Sullivan, K. A. 1986. Influence of prey distribution on aggression on ruddy turnstones. Condor 88:376–378.

Takekawa, J. Y., and N. Warnock. 2000. Long-billed dowitcher (□i□nodro□us scolo□aceus). Pages 1–20 in A. Poole and F. Gill, editors. The birds of North America, No. 493. Academy of Natural Sciences, Philadelphia, and The American Ornithologists' Union, Washington D. C.

Thomas, K., R. G. Kvitek, and C. Bretz. 2003. Effects of human activity on the foraging behavior of sanderlings □alidris alba. Biological Conservation 109:67-71.

*Truitt, B. R., B. D. Watts, B. L. Brown, and W. Dunstan. 2001. Red knot densities and invertebrate prey availability on the Virginia barrier islands. Wader Study Group Bulletin 95:12 (abstract).

Tsipoura, N., and J. Burger. 1999. Shorebird diet during spring migration stopover on Delaware Bay. Condor 101:635-644.

Underhill, L. G., R. P. Prŷs-Jones, E. E. Syroechkovski, Jr., N. M. Groen, V. Karpov, H. G. Lappo, M. W. J. Van Roomen, A. Rybkin, H. Schekkerman, H. Spiekman, and R. W. Summers. 1993. Breeding of waders (Charadrii) and Brent Geese *Branta bernicla bernicla* at Pronchishcheva Lake, northeastern Taimyr, Russia, in a peak and a decreasing lemming year. Ibis 135:277–292.

*U. S. Army Corps of Engineers. 1991. Delaware Bay coastline, New Jersey and Delaware — reconnaissance report. Unpublished report, Philadelphia, Pennsylvania.

*U. S. Army Corps of Engineers. 1997. Villas and vicinity, NJ — interim feasibility study, draft feasibility report and environmental assessment. Unpublished report, Philadelphia, Pennsylvania.

*U. S. Fish and Wildlife Service. 2002. Birds of conservation concern 2002. Unpublished report, U. S. Fish and Wildlife Service, Division of Migratory Bird Management, Arlington, Virginia. 99 pp.

Walls, E. A., J. Berkson, and S. A. Smith. 2002. The horseshoe crab, □i□ulus □oly□he□us: 200 million years of existence, 100 years of study. Reviews in Fisheries Science 10:39-73.

Warnock, N., and R. E. Gill, Jr. 1996. Dunlin (□alidris al□ina). Pages 1–24 in A. Poole and F. Gill, editors. The birds of North America, No. 203. Academy of Natural Sciences, Philadelphia, and The American Ornithologists' Union, Washington D. C.

*Weber, R. G. 2001. Horseshoe crab egg densities observed on six Delaware beaches in 2001. Unpublished report, Delaware National Estuarine Research Reserve, Dover, Delaware. 24 pp.

*Weber, R. G. 2002. Preconstruction horseshoe crab egg density monitoring and habitat availability at Kelly Island, Port Mahon, and Broadkill Beach study areas, Delaware. Unpublished report, Delaware National Estuarine Research Reserve, Dover, Delaware. 23 pp.

West, A. D., J. D. Goss-Custard, R. A. Stillman, R. W. G. Caldow, S. E. A. le V. dit Durell, and S. McGrorty. 2002. Predicting the impacts of disturbance on shorebird mortality using a behavior-based model. Biological Conservation 106:319–328.

Wilson, J. R., A. A. F. Rodrigues, and D. M. Graham. 1998. Red knots (□*alidris canutus ru*□*a*) and other shorebirds on the north central coast of Brazil in April and May 1997. Wader Study Group Bulletin 85:41–45.

Woodard, J. C., D. J. Forrester, F. H. White, J. M. Gaskin, and N. P. Thompson 1977. An epizootic among knots (□*alidris canutus*) in Florida. I. Disease syndrome, histology and transmission studies. Veterinary Pathology 14:338-350.

Zöckler, C., and I. Lysenko. 2000. Water birds on the edge. World Conservation Monitoring Center, World Conservation Press, Cambridge, U. K. 20 pp.

14.0. TABLES

Table 4.1. Reference period landings, quotas, and annual harvest of horseshoe crabs in Atlantic coast states (Atlantic States Marine Fisheries Commission, Horseshoe Crab Technical Committee, unpublished data).

	1995–97 reference	Quota[1] (-25%)	1998	1999	2000	2001	2002[2]
Maine	13,500	13,500	13,500	1,500	1,391	100	0
New Hampshire	350	350	200	350	180	0	120
Massachusetts	440,503	330,377	400,000	545,715	272,930	134,143	138,613
Rhode Island	26,053	26,053	0	26,053	13,809	3,490	3,886
Connecticut	64,919	48,689	34,583	45,050	15,921	11,508	32,080
New York	488,362	366,272	352,462	394,026	628,442	126,336	177,052
New Jersey	604,049	453,037	241,456	297,680	398,629	261,239	281,134
Pennsylvania	0	-	75,000	-	0	0	0
Delaware	482,401	361,801	479,634	402,913	248,938	243,489	298,318
Maryland	613,225	459,919	114,458	134,068	152,275	170,653	278,211
Potomac River Fisheries Commission	0	-	-	-	0	0	0
District of Columbia	0	-	-	-	0	0	0
Virginia	203,326	152,495	1,015,700	650,640	145,465	48,880	36,525
North Carolina	24,036	24,036	24,036	25,602	14,973	9,130	11,115
South Carolina	0	-	-	-	0	0	0
Georgia	29,312	29,312	-	29,312	0	0	0
Florida	9,455	9,455	5,920	11,505	10,462	0	200
Total landings			2,756,949	2,564,414	1,903,415	1,008,968	1,257,254
% reduction total			8	15	37	66	58
% reduction New Jersey			60	51	34	57	53
% reduction Delaware			1	16	48	49	38
% reduction Maryland			81	78	75	72	55

[1] States that qualify for *de □ini□is* status are not required to reduce landings by 25%.
[2] 2002 harvest information in incomplete for a number of states.

Table 4.2. Changes in mean captures of horseshoe crabs (geometric means of catch per unit effort) on trawl surveys in Delaware Bay and along the Atlantic coast (National Marine Fisheries Service fall trawl survey). Periods were selected to correspond to initiation of intensive work on shorebirds in Delaware Bay (Andres analysis; see Figure 1–3). Standard errors only include among-year variance.

Survey	Period	mean ± SE	n	t	df[1]	□
30-foot trawl (all crabs)	1990–1996	3.57 ± 0.80	7	-2.99	8	<0.025
	1997–2002	1.09 ± 0.24	6			
16-foot trawl (<160 mm)	1992–1996	0.48 ± 0.09	5	-1.95	10	<0.09
	1997–2002	0.25 ± 0.07	6			
16-foot trawl (young-of-the-year)	1992–1996	0.41 ± 0.15	5	-1.80	5	<0.14
	1997–2002	0.13 ± 0.04	6			
NMFS fall trawl	1990–1996	0.29 ± 0.04	7	-1.55	10	<0.16
	1997–2000	0.20 ± 0.04	4			

[1] degrees of freedom calculated from Sattherwaite's method (Snedecor and Cochran 1980:97)

Table 5.1. Coarse population estimates of North American-breeding shorebirds from the late 1980s/early 1990s (Morrison et al. 2001). Five levels of confidence (low, low-moderate, moderate, moderate-high, high) in the data used to generate population estimates was scored for each species.

Species	subspecies	North America	Eastern NA	Confidence
Ruddy Turnstone	□□*i*□□*orinella*	180,000	138,600	moderate
Red Knot	□□ *c* □*a*	170,000?	150,000	moderate
Sanderling	□	300,000	116,000	low-moderate
Semipalmated Sandpiper	□	3,500,000	994,600	low-moderate
Least Sandpiper	□	600,000	101,900	low
Dunlin	□□ *a*□ *hudsia*	225,000	138,300	low-moderate
Short-billed Dowitcher	□□g□*griseus*	110,000	110,000	low-moderate
Long-billed Dowitcher	□	500,000	11,300	low

Table 5.2. Annual population size and variability of red knots in the western Atlantic flyway. Estimates derived from mark re-sighting data (Harrington 2002*).

	1981	1982	1983	1985	1986	1987	1988	1989	1990
Mean	212,885	163,563	125,992	157,884	181,778	148,195	167,523	142,983	59,215
Std. dev.	49,576	35,755	30,777	47,804	37,738	53,739	47,364	50,305	16,085

Table 5.3. Aerial survey counts of red knots from southern South America (Morrison and Ross 1989a, Morrison et al. unpublished data).

Year	Bahia Lomas, Chile	Tierra del Fuego, Argentina/Chile	Tierra del Fuego/Patagonia
1982/85	42,762	53,232	67,496
2000	45,705	51,255	–
2001	29,745	–	–
2002	22,172	27,242	29,271

Table 5.4. Maximum counts of shorebirds made on spring aerial surveys of Delaware Bay beaches, 1986-2002 (Niles and Clark, unpublished data).

	Ruddy turnstone	Red knot	Sanderling	Semipalmated Sandpiper	Dunlin	Dowitcher spp.
1986	88,234	58,156	16,193	285,802	8,054	166
1987	68,958	38,790	28,625	93,600	8,630	1,748
1988	58,390	34,750	41,055	177,110	2,030	2,980
1989	108,120	95,490	6,252	86,712	2,300	265
1990	32,301	45,860	5,378	48,185	2,875	1,130
1991	42,020	27,280	5,305	68,300	3,480	1,136
1992	53,930	25,595	7,330	42,630	11,245	6,335
1993	64,985	44,000	10,390	91,080	4,875	2,875
1994	80,795	52,055	9,955	95,180	12,165	5,045
1995	70,370	38,600	10,130	81,235	6,385	3,675
1996	47,115	19,445	8,355	41,190	8,740	8,330
1997	69,340	41,855	15,455	74,825	4,880	3,955
1998	101,660	50,360	23,520	67,745	16,305	6,830
1999	87,605	49,805	10,005	83,695	31,345	11,415
2000	69,000	43,145	20,815	100,635	39,935	10,185
2001	86,365	36,125	21,830	188,925	45,080	13,375
2002	64,690	31,695	13,835	51,320	32,305	13,000

Table 5.5. Difference in mean maximum counts of shorebirds made on spring aerial surveys of Delaware Bay between 1986-1996 and 1997-2002 (Niles and Clark unpublished data; Andres analysis).

| | Delaware Bay peak counts between periods | | | | | Kendall's trend | |
| | 1986-1996 | 1997-2002 | | | | (1997–2002) | |
	mean ± SE	mean ± SE	t-value	$\square$	df[1]	correlation coef.	$\square$
Red Knot	43,638 ± 6,239	42,164 ± 3,015	-0.21	>0.20	15	-0.60	0.068
Ruddy Turnstone	65,020 ± 6,590	79,777 ± 5,877	1.67	>0.40	16	0.47	0.136
Sanderling	13,543 ± 3,410	17,577 ± 2,158	0.10	>0.40	16	0.07	0.500
Semipalmated Sandpiper	101,002 ± 21,652	94,524 ± 20,032	-0.22	>0.40	16	-0.20	0.360
Dunlin	6,434 ± 1,083	28,308 ± 6,150	3.50	<0.025	6	0.73	0.028
Dowitcher spp.	3,062 ± 787	9,793 ± 1,514	3.95	>0.40	9	0.73	0.028

[1] degrees of freedom calculated from Satterthwaite's method (Snedecor and Cochran 1980:97).

Table 5.6. Trends of selected shorebirds from analysis of International Shorebird Survey (ISS) data collected in eastern North America (Bart et al. 2002*), Maritime Shorebird Survey (MSS) data (Morrison and Hicklin 2001*), and Quebec checklist data collected during fall migration (Aubry and Cotter 2001*).

| | Eastern North America | | Canadian MSS (adults) | | | | Quebec fall migration checklists | | |
| | ISS (1976–2000) | | 1970s – 1990s | | 1980s – 1990s | | | | |
	% change	□	trend[1]	□	trend[1]	□	occurrence	trend	□
Red Knot	-1.65	>0.10	neg	<0.01	neg	<0.01	uncommon	neg	≤0.05
Ruddy Turnstone	+1.05	>0.10	+/-	>0.10	+/-	>0.10	common	neg	≤0.05
Sanderling	-4.76	<0.01	+/-	>0.10	+/-	>0.10	common	+/-	>0.10
Semipalmated Sandpiper	-3.88	<0.05	neg	<0.01	neg	<0.10	common	neg	≤0.05
Least Sandpiper	-6.90	<0.05	neg	<0.001	+/-	>0.10	common	+/-	>0.10
Dunlin	+0.21	>0.10	neg	<0.05	neg	<0.05	common	+/-	>0.10
Short-billed Dowitcher	+1.26	>0.10	neg	<0.001	neg	<0.001	uncommon	+/-	>0.10
Long-billed Dowitcher	+0.47	>0.10	–	–	–	–	rare	–	–

[1] trends are indicated as negative (neg), positive (pos), or stable (+/-).

Table 6.1   Percentage of total numbers of birds observed on aerial surveys of Delaware Bay beaches relative to all International Shorebird Surveys (ISS) observations on the U. S. Atlantic coast (Harrington 2002*) and to coarse population estimates for the Atlantic flyway (see Table 5.1).

| Season | % in Delaware Bay relative to | |
Species	ISS data	coarse population estimates
Southward migration		
Ruddy Turnstone	2.3	0.2
Red Knot	<0.1	<0.1
Sanderling	0.4	0.4
Semipalmated Sandpiper	8.7[1]	2.5
Least Sandpiper		
Dunlin	5.6	3.8
Short-billed Dowitcher	10.9[2]	8.1
Long-billed Dowitcher		
Northward migration		
Ruddy Turnstone	47.5	78.0
Red Knot	40.2	63.7
Sanderling	34.4	35.4
Semipalmated Sandpiper	50.0[1]	28.7[2]
Least Sandpiper		
Dunlin	39.7	32.6
Short-billed Dowitcher	23.2[3]	12.2
Long-billed Dowitcher		

[1] includes all small □alidris sandpipers but is mainly semipalmated sandpipers.
[2] 53.2% if just the Bay of Fundy of Fundy population is included (Hicklin 1997).
[3] includes both dowitcher species but is mainly short-billed dowitchers.

Table 7.1. Average number of shorebirds observed in marine and non-marine habitats on International Shorebird Surveys (ISS) along the Atlantic coast, United States (Harrington 2002*).

Season	Average count		Prominent	
Species	marine	non-marine	habitat	p - value
Southward migration	$n = 278$ sites	$n = 323$ sites		
Ruddy Turnstone	7.29	0.22	marine	<0.001
Red Knot	22.33	0.05	marine	<0.001
Sanderling	84.63	0.99	marine	<0.001
Semipalmated Sandpiper	100.55	19.55	marine	<0.001
Least Sandpiper	16.17	25.08		>0.05
Dunlin	24.70	2.76	marine	<0.001
Short-billed Dowitcher	22.70	6.74	marine	<0.01
Long-billed Dowitcher	1.25	19.19		>0.05
Northward migration	$n = 199$ sites	$n = 322$ sites		
Ruddy Turnstone	31.90	1.55	marine	<0.01
Red Knot	24.45	2.04	marine	<0.001
Sanderling	52.92	3.37	marine	<0.001
Semipalmated Sandpiper	71.28	40.32		>0.05
Least Sandpiper	19.89	17.51		>0.05
Dunlin	119.01	33.42	marine	<0.001
Short-billed Dowitcher	24.68	4.70	marine	<0.01
Long-billed Dowitcher	5.56	4.47		>0.05

Table 7.2. Qualitative assessment of use of Delaware beaches by ruddy turnstones and red knots during spring migration (Carter 2002*).

Delaware beach	Ruddy turnstone	Red knot
Port Mahon	EH[1]	R[2]
Pickering Beach	H[3]	R
Kitts Hummock	EH	H
St. Jones River	EH	EH
Bowers Beach	EH	H
South Bowers	EH	EH
Greco Canal Breach	M[4]	H
Mispillion Harbor	EH	EH
Slaughter Beach	H	H

[1] extremely high use - large flocks at all weather conditions.
[2] occasional use - some individuals, not regular.
[3] high use - large flocks in mild weather conditions.
[4] moderate use - occasional large flocks intermittently.

Table 8.1. Density of horseshoe crab eggs (eggs/m^2) on Delaware and New Jersey beaches in 1999 (Pooler et al. 2003).

		25–26 May				14–15 June			
State		shallow (0-5 cm)		deep (0-20 cm)		shallow (0-5 cm)		deep (0-20 cm)	
	Beach	mean	SE	mean	SE	mean	SE	mean	SE
Delaware									
	Broadkill	0	0	764	749	611	183	51,795	30,772
	Prime Hook	102	41	41,711	38,793	3,769	1,049	114,031	57,112
	Fowler	51	25	917	331	1,375	621	107,614	59,364
	Slaughter	5,959	1,370	414,975	94,749	21,238	2,725	338,427	49,814
	Big Stone	51	25	5,755	2,592	357	270	12,325	7,268
	North Bowers	11,714	3,305	486,984	119,267	53,527	11,989	203,922	36,063
	Kitts Hummock	13,445	4,192	165,572	40,046	7,741	2,796	63,560	22,378
	Woodland	255	87	51	31	3,565	1,874	31,016	15,152
New Jersey									
	North Cape May	153	127	0	0	255	168	357	188
	South Cape Shore Lab	12,987	438	552,790	71,449	2,292	413	712,607	73,354
	Highs	1,070	362	574,792	49,397	2,241	479	741,943	88,516
	Kimbles	4,940	2,445	795,164	145,822	866	280	513,371	53,797
	Reeds	1,171	265	275,224	40,693	9,269	1,283	238,351	31,918
	Raybins	1,783	973	33,512	22,348	51	31	3,412	2,327
	Fortescue	1,019	219	328,954	55,366	10,492	1,961	237,179	98,620
	Sea Breeze	14,006	4,049	176,879	48,230	102	46	1,579	1,024

Table 8.2. Horseshoe crab egg densities (eggs/m^2) and percentage of eggs found in shallow (0–5 cm) sediments on Delaware beaches in 2001 (Weber 2001*).

	9–11 May			25 May
Beach	eggs/m^2	% shallow		eggs/m^2
Mispillion	502,000	23		530,000
St. Jones	121,000	12		–
Port Mahon	114,000	24		133,000
Old Pickering	60,000	8		21,000
Kitts Hummock	45,000	9		24,000
New Pickering	18,000	6		9,000
North Bowers	6,000	4		1,000
Kelly Island	873	50		13,000

Table 9.1. Numbers of gulls observed during aerial surveys of Delaware Bay beaches of New Jersey (Niles, unpublished data).

	31 May 1990	29 May 1991	19 May 1992	26 May 2002
Laughing gull	6,640	23,150	29,780	10,125
Herring/Black-backed gull	11,209	14,279	11,412	2,579
All gull species	17,849	37,429	43,644	12,704

Table 9.2. Time shorebirds were engaged in behaviors associated with foraging when the nearest neighbor was a gull or another shorebird in Delaware Bay 2002 (Burger et al. 2003*).

	Focal species		
	red knot	ruddy turnstone	sanderling
Pecks			
sample size	177	808	145
overall mean	18.53 ± 0.98	26.79 ± 0.47	24.43 ± 1.21
shorebird nearest neighbor	19.71 ± 1.20	28.97 ± 0.58	25.30 ± 1.29
gull nearest neighbor	14.74 ± 1.29	22.36 ± 0.72	15.69 ± 1.46
Kruskal-Wallis χ^2 (P)	2.61 (>0.05)	45.0 (0.0001)	5.45 (0.02)
Foraging			
sample size	297	1,259	246
overall mean	19.85 ± 0.52	22.95 ± 0.22	21.59 ± 0.54

shorebird nearest neighbor	20.25 ± 0.57	24.03 ± 0.24	21.81 ± 0.56
gull nearest neighbor	17.63 ± 1.28	19.91 ± 0.45	18.50 ± 2.35
Kruskal-Wallis χ^2 (P)	3.82 (0.05)	78.3 (0.0001)	2.23 (>0.05)
Vigilant			
sample size	297	1,259	245
overall mean	3.62 ± 0.35	2.55 ± 0.14	1.47 ± 0.24
shorebird nearest neighbor	3.12 ± 0.36	1.88 ± 0.14	1.50 ± 0.25
gull nearest neighbor	6.33 ± 1.02	4.44 ± 0.34	1.07 ± 0.70
Kruskal-Wallis χ^2 (P)	12.0 (0.0005)	80.5 (0.0001)	0.03 (>0.05)
Aggressive interactions			
sample size	290	1,232	245
overall mean	0.18 ± 0.03	0.47 ± 0.03	0.34 ± 0.05

shorebird nearest neighbor	0.12 ± 0.03	0.45 ± 0.03	0.33 ± 0.05
gull nearest neighbor	0.48 ± 0.14	0.53 ± 0.05	0.47 ± 0.29
Kruskal-Wallis χ^2 (P)	9.73 (0.002)	9.81 (0.002)	0.001 (>0.05)

Table 10.1. Energetic requirements of shorebirds during spring migration in Delaware Bay (Casto and Myers 1993; Andres adjustments).

	Lean mass (g)	BMR (kJ/hr)	Total energy expenditure[1] (kJ)	Energy in fat (kJ)[2]	% fat	cost of fat (kJ)[3]	Total energy need of an individual (expend.*fat cost)	Population size[4]	Total energy need for the population (kJ*10^8)	Total energy consumption (kJ*10^8)[5]	Eggs ingested (metric tons)[6]
Ruddy Turnstone	101	3.42	3,488	3,979	50	4,522	8,010	101,700	8.15	11.64	113.5
Red Knot	134	4.23	4,314	4,320	45	4,909	9,223	50,400	4.65	6.64	64.8
Semipalmated Sandpiper	25	1.23	1,254	657	40	746	2,001	188,900	3.78	5.40	52.7
Sanderling	50	2.05	2,091	4,597	70	5,223	7,314	23,500	1.72	2.46	24.0
Dowitcher spp.	100	3.39	3,458	2,627	40	2,985	6,443	45,100	2.91	4.15	40.5
Dunlin	55	2.19	2,234	1,447	40	1,642	3,875	13,400	0.52	0.74	7.2

[1] 2.5*BMR*(24 hours)*(17 days).
[2] 39.5 kJ/g of fat.
[3] 88% efficiency in depositing fat.
[4] highest maximum count 1997–2002.
[5] 70% assimilation efficiency.
[6] 10.25 kJ/g caloric equivalent of eggs.

Table 11.1. Proportion of red knot catches (those >50 birds) at Mispillion Harbor, Slaughter Beach, Cook's Beach and Reed's Beach in Delaware Bay from 1997 to 2002 (Robinson et Al. 2003*).

	1997	1998	1999	2000	2001	2002
Total number caught	893	1,086	2,431	1,145	2,234	1,349
% at Mispillion, Slaughter, Cook's, and Reed's	1.00	0.73	0.68	0.36	0.74	0.95

Table 11.2. Proportion of of red knot captures among time periods in Delaware Bay, 1997–2002 (Robinson et al. 2003*).

	10–14 May	15–19 May	20–24 May	25–30 May	Total caught
1997	0.00	0.00	0.79	0.21	893
1998	0.27	0.21	0.26	0.26	1,086
1999	0.18	0.13	0.24	0.45	2,431
2000	0.24	0.25	0.12	0.38	1,145
2001	0.09	0.13	0.47	0.31	2,234
2002	0.32	0.11	0.33	0.24	1,349

Table 11.3. Weekly counts of red knots, ruddy turnstones, and sanderlings made on aerial surveys (May–June) of Delaware Bay between 1997 and 2002 (Niles et al., unpublished data).

week	1997	1998	1999	2000	2001	2002
Red Knot						
1	1721	787	0	0	3740	660
2	6445	16615	6670	765	23415	10170
3	21475	48945	18660	22960	36125	27330
4	41855	50360	49805	43145	32350	31695
5	9510	2920	10550	7160	7540	2323
Ruddy Turnstone						
1	3170	1100	170	185	935	4380
2	8690	11050	7960	6580	37705	31445
3	34465	47535	52610	43240	86365	56625
4	69340	101660	87640	69000	79310	64690
5	29537	16850	42685	36595	58840	6563
Sanderling						
1	2985	2880	3950	2526	3185	2779
2	3495	8950	6405	4640	8555	4540
3	8550	17715	7970	13510	21830	13765
4	15455	23520	9995	20815	8110	7872
5	3365	5400	10005	10050	12465	1980

Table 11.4 . The daily crude rate of mass gain of shorebirds (sample size) caught May 14 to May 28, 1997–2002 in Delaware and New Jersey (Niles et al. 2003*).

	Red knot			Ruddy turnstone			Sanderling	
	Delaware	New Jersey		Delaware	New Jersey		Delaware	New Jersey
1997	10.31 (876)	–		–	1.14 (659)		–	1.93 (305)
1998	7.32 (433)	5.62 (305)		5.89 (530)	3.53 (771)		1.21 (108)	1.04 (348)
1999	2.94 (996)	3.02 (830)		1.02 (411)	3.72 (794)		0.25 (53)	1.23 (1,267)
2000	2.19 (669)	4.38 (344)		3.32 (393)	3.59 (811)		0.13 (60)	1.09 (423)
2001	4.22 (1,241)	4.76 (518)		3.35 (414)	3.23 (1,713)		1.66 (38)	1.29 (899)
2002	2.33 (745)	2.62 (83)		3.32 (671)	3.20 (463)		1.35 (92)	2.09 (491)

Table 11.5 Regression coefficients (b1) of best fit lines describing relationships between Julian date and mean fat mass of semipalmated sandpiper cohorts captured during spring migration stopovers along New Jersey's Delaware Bay coast. For each year, linear regression analyses were conducted for cohorts captured at Thompsons Beach only, and for Thompsons and Raybins Beaches combined. Data sets were truncated to include only cohorts captured on or after 17-18 May (Julian day 138). Analyses either assessed mean fat mass gain through the day of last capture, typically during the first week of June, or were truncated to describe the period of maximum fat mass gain. Analysis of covariance detected significant differences among regression coefficients within each analysis category. Students t-tests were used to determine pairwise differences between $\beta 1$ coefficients within each category and controlled for experimentwise error related to multiple comparisons by using Bonferroni corrections for a. Overall, ten comparisons were made, resulting in an adjusted a of 0.005. Within analysis categories, values in "$\beta 1$" columns with the same letter are not statistically different.

| Year | All capture days ≥day 138 | | | | Period of maximum gain | | | |
	$\beta 1$	SE	$\square\square$	period end (Julian day)	b1	SE	$\square^2$	period end (Julian day)
Thompson's Beach								
1996	1.14a	0.10	0.95	150	1.18a	0.12	0.91	149
1997	0.49b	0.05	0.87	156	0.58b	0.06	0.89	151
2000	0.18c	0.05	0.46	154	0.18c	0.05	0.46	152
2001	0.53bd	0.08	0.85	151	0.53bd	0.08	0.85	151
2002	0.08*bcd	0.19	0.08	147	0.60abcd	0.06	0.97	144
Thompson's/Raybins Beaches								
1996	0.9294a	0.0986	0.86	153	1.1829a	0.1194	0.91	149
1997	0.4891b	0.0502	0.87	156	0.5785b	0.0575	0.89	151
2000	0.3239b	0.0651	0.58	157	0.3239b	0.0651	0.58	157
2001	0.5323ab	0.0792	0.85	151	0.5323b	0.0792	0.85	151
2002	0.2874b	0.0755	0.49	156	0.3846b	0.1021	0.54	152

[1] $\beta 1$ not statistically significant

15.0. FIGURES

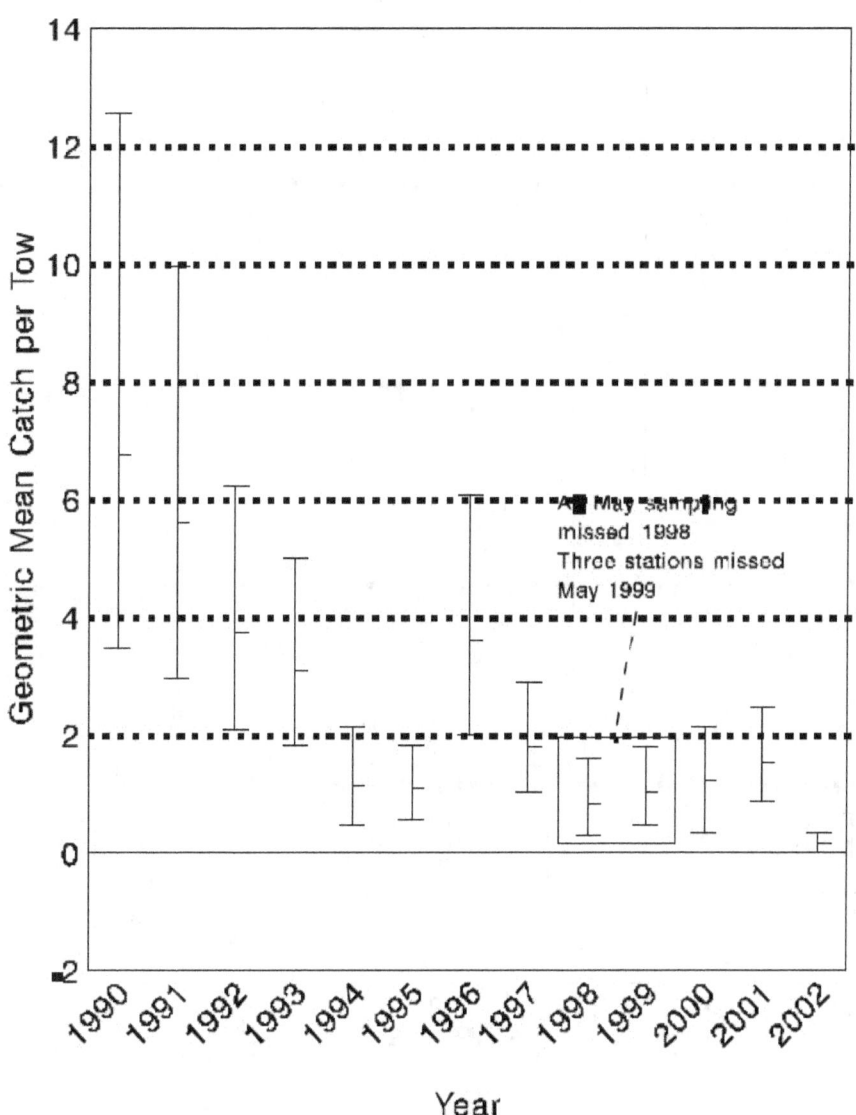

Figure 1. Geometric mean, and 95% confidence intervals, of catch of all horseshoe crabs in the Delaware 30-foot trawl survey, 1990–2002 (S. Michels, unpublished data).

Horseshoe Crab Juvenile (<160mm) Index
16-Foot Trawl

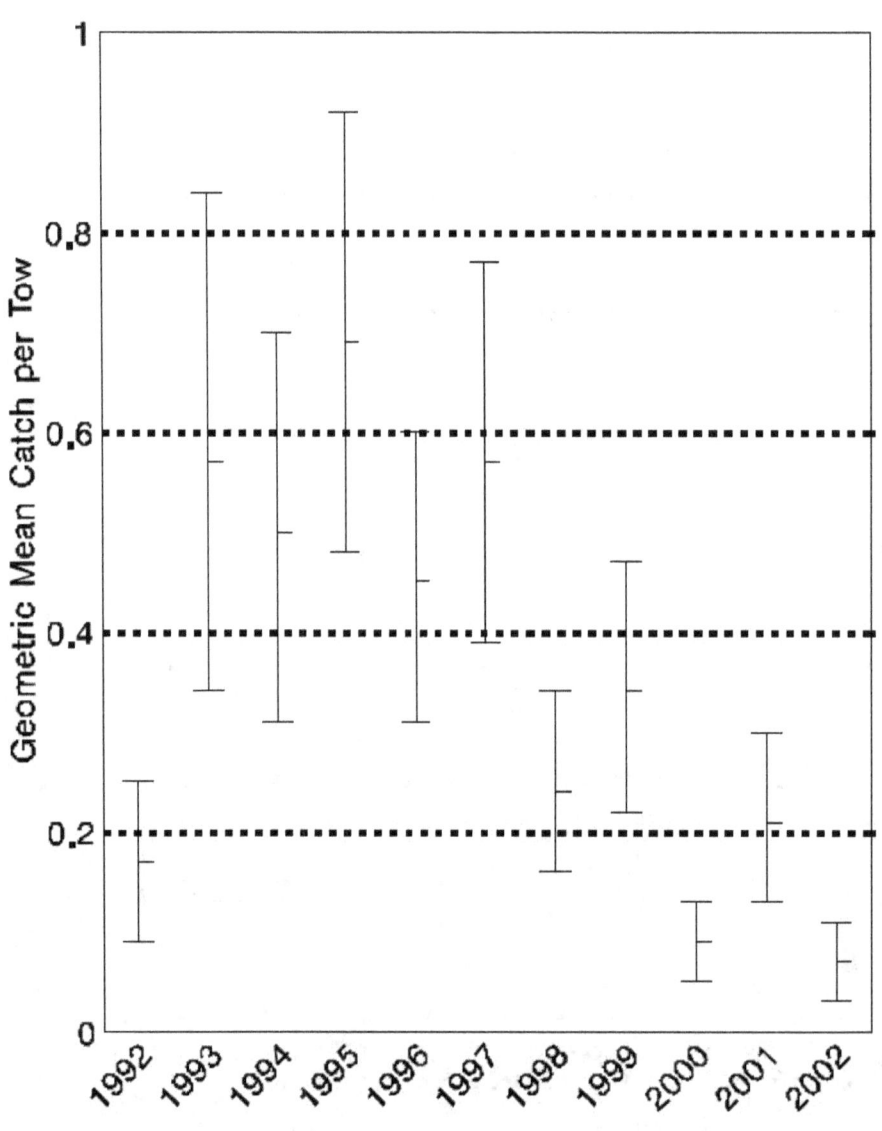

Figure 2. Geometric mean, and 95% confidence intervals, of catch of juvenile (<160mm) horseshoe crabs in the Delaware 16-foot trawl survey, 1992–2002 (S. Michels, unpublished data).

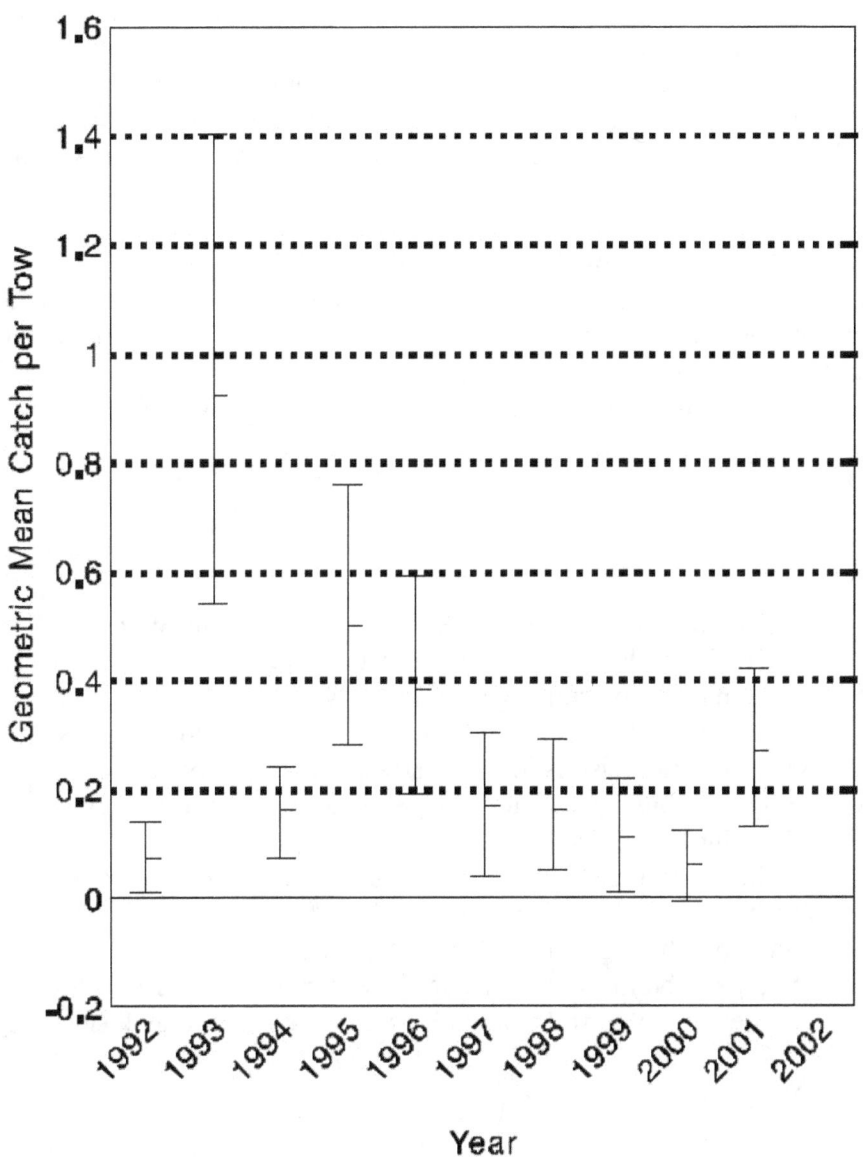

Figure 3. Geometric mean, and 95% confidence intervals, of catch of young-of-the-year horseshoe crabs in the Delaware 16-foot trawl survey, 1992–2002 (S. Michels, unpublished data).

C. Shorebird Technical Committee Terms of Reference – 2002

1.0. CHARGE AND IMMEDIATE ACTIONS

The purpose of the Shorebird Technical Committee (SBTC) is to provide technical advice to the Horseshoe Crab Fishery Management Board of the Atlantic States Marine Fisheries Commission on how horseshoe crab management actions might affect shorebird populations. The long-term tenure of the SBTC will be determined by the need to provide technical support to the Management Board. Therefore, these Terms of Reference will be reviewed annually and revised as needed.

The immediate task of the SBTC is to oversee the production of a peer-reviewed report that synthesizes current literature and data on the status of shorebirds in Delaware Bay and to determine their energetic dependency on horseshoe crab eggs. The SBTC will review the report and draft a summary and recommendations from the results. The SBTC will also identify and prioritize research and monitoring needed for the conservation of Delaware Bay's shorebirds.

2.0. MEMBERSHIP

2.1. Members

Karen Bennett	Shorebird biologist, Delaware Division of Fish and Wildlife
Gregory Breese	Shorebird biologist, U. S. Fish and Wildlife Service
Joanna Burger	Shorebird biologist, Rutgers University
David Carter	Shorebird biologist, Delaware Coastal Management Program
Robert Gorrell	Fisheries biologist, National Marine Fisheries Service
Brian Harrington	Shorebird biologist, Manomet Center for Conservation Sciences
Marshall Howe	Shorebird biologist, U. S. Geological Survey
Stewart Michels	Fisheries biologist, Horseshoe Crab Technical Committee
Mike Millard	Fisheries biologist, U. S. Fish and Wildlife Service
David Mizrahi	Shorebird biologist, New Jersey Audubon Society
Lawrence Niles	Shorebird biologist, New Jersey Division of Fish and Wildlife
Nellie Tsipoura	Shorebird biologist, National Resource Defense Council (formerly)

2.2. Official Observers

Alan Baker	Shorebird biologist, Royal Ontario Museum
Carrie Selberg/Brad Spear	ASMFC Horseshoe Crab Fishery Management Plan Coordinator

2.3. Coordinator/Facilitator

Brad Andres	Shorebird biologist, U. S. Fish and Wildlife Service

3.0. Operations

The U. S. Fish and Wildlife Service will coordinate and facilitate operation of the SBTC and will be responsible for setting meeting agendas, distributing information, and ensuring actions identified by the SBTC are implemented. Immediate responsibility of coordination and facilitation of the SBTC lies with the National Shorebird Coordinator within the Division of Migratory Bird Management. Administration of the SBTC may be transferred to the regional U. S. Fish and Wildlife Service office in the future.

Agreement on actions taken by the SBTC will be reached by consensus. If a consensus opinion can not be reached, majority and minority opinions will be drafted. Weight of the support of each opinion will be noted (e.g., 9 of 11 members present). Official observers, who are agreed on by members, can participate in discussions, but will not draft committee opinions or be included in enumeration of opinion support. A quorum of 8 of 11 members is needed to conduct official SBTC business. Alternates can be chosen to represent members at meetings. Changes to the Terms of Reference will be accepted by members as above.

SBTC members are expected to attend 1-3 meetings annually and to provide a thorough review of the synthesis report. Meetings are open, but discussion can be limited to SBTC members and official observers. State and federal management agencies are expected to cover staff and travel costs to attend meetings. Non-governmental and university participants will be compensated for travel expenses. A representative of the State of Maryland may be added to the SBTC in the future.

4.0. Budgets

4.1. FY2002 (1 Oct 2001 - 30 Sep 2002)

Travel to committee meetings (2)	$4,000 (NJ DFW)
Peer Review contracts	$6,000 (DE DNREC)
Contracts to report authors	$25,000 (US FWS)

4.2. FY2003

Travel to committee meetings (2)	$6,000 (US FWS)
Peer Review travel	$12,000 (4K-DE DNREC; 6K-NJ DFW; 2K-US FWS)

4.3. FY2004 and annually thereafter

Travel to committee meetings (2)	$6,000 (US FWS)

5.0. Addresses, Phone Numbers, and E-mails of SBTC Members and Observers

Brad A. Andres
National Shorebird Coordinator
U.S. Fish and Wildlife Service
Division of Migratory Bird Management
4401 North Fairfax Drive, MBSP 4107
Arlington, VA 22203
Phone: 703-358-1828; fax: 2217
E-mail: Brad_Andres@fws.gov

Allan Baker
Head
Centre for Biodiversity and Conservation Biology
Royal Ontario Museum
100 Queen's Park
Toronto, Ontario, Canada M5S 2C6
Phone: 416-586-5520; fax:
E-mail: allanb@rom.on.ca

Karen Bennett
Program Manager
Delaware Division of Fish and Wildlife
Natural Heritage Program/Nongame and Endangered Species Program
4876 Hay Point Landing Rd.
Smyrna, DE 19977
Phone: 302-653-2880; fax: 302-653-3431
E-mail: karen.bennett@state.de.us

Gregory Breese
Senior Staff Biologist
Delaware Bay Estuary Project
U. S. Fish and Wildlife Service
2610 Whitehall Neck Road
Smyrna, DE 19977
Phone: 302-653-9152; fax: 9421
E-mail: Gregory_Breese@fws.gov

Joanna Burger
Professor
Nelson Biology Lab
Rutgers University
604 Allison Road
Piscataway, NJ 08854-8082
Phone: 732-445-4318; fax:
E-mail: burger@biology.rutgers.edu

David Carter
Environmental Program Manager II
Division of Soil and Water Conservation
Delaware Department of Natural Resources and Environmental Control
89 Kings Highway
Dover, DE 19901
Phone: 302-739-3451; fax: 2048
E-mail: dcarter@dnrec.state.de.us

Robert Gorrell
Fishery Biologist
Office of Sustainable Fisheries
National Marine Fisheries Service
1315 East West Highway, #13463
Silver Spring, MD 20910
Phone: 301-713-2341 ext. 150; fax: 9113
E-mail: Robert.Gorrell@noaa.gov

Brian Harrington
Senior Scientist
Manomet Center for Conservation Sciences
PO Box 1770
Manomet, Massachusetts 02345
Phone: 508-224-6521; fax: 9220
E-mail: bharr@manomet.org

Marshall Howe
Chief, Monitoring Program
Patuxent Wildlife Research Center
U. S. Geological Survey
12100 Beech Forest Road,
Laurel, MD 20708-4038
Phone: 301-497-5858; fax: 5784
E-mail: Marshall_Howe@usgs.gov

Stewart Michels
Chair, Horseshoe Crab Technical Committee
Fisheries Section
Delaware Division of Fish and Wildlife
89 Kings Highway
Dover, DE 19901
Phone: 302-739-4782; fax: 6780
E-mail: Stewart.Michels@state.de.us

Mike Millard
Fishery Ecologist
Northeast Fishery Center
U. S. Fish and Wildlife Service
308 Washington Ave.
Lamar, PA 16848
Phone: 570-726-4247; fax: 2416
E-mail: Mike_Millard@fws.gov

David Mizrahi
Vice President for Research
Cape May Bird Observatory
New Jersey Audubon Society
600 Route 47 North
Cape May Court House, NJ 08210
Phone: 609-861-0700; fax: 1651
E-mail: dmizrahi@njaudubon.org

Lawrence Niles
Chief
Endangered and Nongame Species Program
New Jersey Division of Fish and Wildlife
P. O. Box 400
Trenton, NJ 08625-0400
Phone: 609-292-9400; fax: 1414
E-mail: lniles@dep.state.nj.us

Carrie Selberg/Braddock Spear
Horseshoe Crab Fishery Management Plan Coordinator
Atlantic States Marine Fisheries Commission
1444 "I" Street, 6th Floor
Washington, DC 20005
Phone: 202-289-6400; fax: 6051
E-mail: cselberg@asmfc.org/bspear@asmfc.org

Nellie Tsipoura
Biologist
Water and Coastal Programs
National Resource Defense Council
40 West 20 Street
New York, NY 10011
Phone: 212-727-4539; fax: 1773
E-mail: ntsipoura@nrdc.org

www.ingramcontent.com/pod-product-compliance
Lightning Source LLC
Chambersburg PA
CBHW080308290526
45790CB00005B/1970